PENGUIN MODERN CLASSICS

Tokyo Express

Seichō Matsumoto was born in 1909 in Fukuoka, Japan. Self-educated, Matsumoto published his first book when he was forty years old and quickly established himself as a master of crime fiction. His exploration of human psychology and Japanese post-war malaise, coupled with the creation of twisting, dark mysteries, made him one of the most acclaimed and best-selling writers in Japan. He received the prestigious Akutagawa Literary Prize in 1950 and the Kikuchi Kan Prize in 1970. He died in 1992.

SEICHŌ MATSUMOTO

Tokyo Express

Translated by JESSE KIRKWOOD

PENGUIN BOOKS

PENGUIN CLASSICS

UK | USA | Canada | Ireland | Australia
India | New Zealand | South Africa

Penguin Books is part of the Penguin Random House group of companies
whose addresses can be found at global.penguinrandomhouse.com

First Japanese edition published by Kobunsha Co. Ltd 1958
Republished in *The Complete Works of Matsumoto Seichō*, Vol. 1, by
Bungeishunju Ltd 1971
This translation first published in Penguin Modern Classics 2022
This edition published 2023

 010

Typeset by Jouve (UK), Milton Keynes
Printed and bound in Great Britain by Clays Ltd, Elcograf S.p.A.

The authorized representative in the EEA is Penguin Random House Ireland,
Morrison Chambers, 32 Nassau Street, Dublin D02 YH68

A CIP catalogue record for this book is available from the British Library

ISBN: 978–0–241–43908–1

www.greenpenguin.co.uk

MIX
Paper | Supporting
responsible forestry
FSC® C018179

Penguin Random House is committed to a
sustainable future for our business, our readers
and our planet. This book is made from Forest
Stewardship Council® certified paper.

Tokyo Express

1. The Witnesses

I

On the evening of the thirteenth of January, Tatsuo Yasuda invited one of his clients to join him at the Koyuki restaurant in Akasaka. His guest was a senior official at one of the government ministries.

Yasuda was the president of a company that sold industrial machinery. The company had grown considerably in recent years, a success it was rumoured to owe to its large number of contracts with the government. This explained why Yasuda often brought important officials like tonight's guest to the Koyuki.

Yasuda liked the restaurant. It wasn't the fanciest in this part of Tokyo, but that was precisely what gave it such an informal, relaxing atmosphere – and the waitresses who served in the private dining rooms were all more than up to the task. Yasuda was considered a good customer. He was happy to splash his cash around – or, as he liked to call it, his 'capital'. His clients were all the type to enjoy this extravagance. Still, no matter how friendly he was to the waitresses, he took care never to reveal much about his guests.

A bribery scandal had been in the news since the previous autumn, centring on a certain government ministry. A number of companies doing business with the ministry were also said to be involved. So far only a few lower-ranking officials had been implicated, but the newspapers were predicting that by spring the scandal would have spread to the ministry's upper echelons.

As a result, Yasuda had become even more discreet about his guests' identities. There were clients he had brought seven or eight times, whom the waitresses knew by affectionate nicknames like

'Ko-san' or 'Wu-san' – and yet, while they realized most of these guests were government officials of some sort, they learned nothing further about them.

In any case, it didn't matter who they were. Yasuda was the one footing the bill. All they needed to do at the Koyuki was keep him happy.

Tatsuo Yasuda was around forty years old, with a broad forehead and a rather sharp nose. He had a dark complexion, kind eyes, and eyebrows so thick they could almost have been painted on. He radiated the easy confidence of an experienced businessman. Despite his popularity with the waitresses, it seemed he never had designs on any of them, instead showing the same friendliness to each.

His designated waitress was Toki, for the simple reason that she had been the one to serve him on his first visit. While they were on good enough terms, it seemed their relationship had never gone beyond the walls of the Koyuki.

Toki was twenty-six but with her beautiful pale skin could easily have passed for twenty. Her large black eyes made quite the impression on guests. When one of them addressed her, she would glance up and flash them a smile she knew they would find enchanting. Her oval face and delicate chin gave her a graceful profile.

It was no surprise, then, that several customers had attempted to seduce her. Rather than living in, the waitresses came into the restaurant at around four every afternoon and headed home sometime after eleven. Sometimes a customer would ambush Toki as she left the restaurant, asking her to meet him under the railway bridge at Shinbashi. She couldn't turn them down flat – they *were* customers after all – so instead would breezily agree to their requests before standing them up three or four times in a row. That way, as Toki was explaining, the penny would usually drop.

'Sometimes they're a little slow on the uptake. One turned up the other day in a rage. Pinched me so hard I practically screamed!'

Still seated, Toki lifted her kimono, revealing to her colleagues a small blueish patch on her pale knee.

'Well, what did you expect, leading him on like that!' said Yasuda, smiling as he tipped back his sake cup. The waitresses knew him well enough that he was privy even to this kind of gossip.

'Say, Ya-san, how come *you* never try it on with us?' asked Yaeko.

'What would be the point? Knowing you lot, you'd only stand me up!'

'Just listen to him! I know your type, Ya-san,' teased Kaneko, another waitress.

'Oh, I don't know what you're implying –'

'It's no use, Kane-chan,' cut in Toki. 'We're all smitten with Mr Yasuda, but he barely even looks at us. I wouldn't waste your time.'

'Hmph!' said Kaneko, flashing a grin.

It was just as Toki had said: the waitresses at the Koyuki were quite taken with Yasuda, and if he'd ever made approaches they would have been well received. His looks and personality made him an irresistible choice.

That evening, after seeing his guest off at the entrance, Yasuda had returned to the private room to relax with a drink. When he turned to Yaeko and her colleague Tomiko and asked, 'By the way, you two – how about I take you out for a meal tomorrow?' they jumped at the offer.

'But what about Toki? Why don't you invite her too?' asked Tomiko, casting her eyes around for her friend, who had left the room on some errand or another.

'Let's make it just the two of you. I'll take Toki another time. I can't have you all skipping out on work.'

This was true. The waitresses were supposed to be at the restaurant by four and would arrive late if they ate out beforehand. It wouldn't do for all three of them to join him.

'That's settled then. I'll see you at three thirty, at the Levante in Yūrakuchō,' said Yasuda, his eyes crinkling as he smiled.

2

When Tomiko walked into the Levante at around three thirty the next day, she found Yasuda drinking a coffee at a table in the back.

He greeted her and gestured to the seat opposite. It felt odd seeing him here, rather than in the usual setting of the restaurant, and she found herself blushing as she sat down.

'Oh, no Yaeko yet?'

'She'll be along any moment,' replied Yasuda with a smile, then ordered her a coffee. A few minutes later, Yaeko walked in, looking similarly bashful. Dressed in kimonos that gave away their profession, the two waitresses stood out from the young couples filling the café.

'What kind of food do you two feel like? How about something Western? Chinese? Maybe tempura, or eel?' asked Yasuda.

'Western food,' they replied simultaneously. It seemed they were already getting their fill of Japanese food at the restaurant.

The three of them left the Levante and headed towards Ginza. The streets weren't too busy at this time of day and, though a cold wind was blowing, the weather was fine. They walked at a leisurely pace, crossing at the corner of Owari-chō towards the Matsuzakaya department store. In stark contrast to the end-of-year holidays two weeks earlier, Ginza was practically deserted.

'Jam-packed on Christmas Eve, wasn't it!' commented one of the waitresses as they walked behind Yasuda. He led them up the steps of the Coq d'Or. The restaurant, too, was almost empty.

'Well, order whatever you like,' said Yasuda once they were seated.

'Oh, don't worry, we'll have anything,' Yaeko and Tomiko replied, out of politeness. But once the menu was in their hands they began debating their options at length. They seemed to be struggling to decide.

Yasuda's eyes darted to his wristwatch. This didn't escape Yaeko, who turned and asked, 'Oh dear, Ya-san – somewhere you need to be?'

'No, not particularly. It's just that I'm off to Kamakura this evening,' replied Yasuda, his hands clasped on the table.

'Oh, we're sorry. Tomiko, we should hurry up and choose!'

And so they finally reached a decision. The meal began with a soup course and took quite a long time to finish. The three of them chatted about this and that. Yasuda seemed to be enjoying himself. When the fruit was served, he glanced again at his watch.

'Time to be heading off?'

'Not quite yet,' replied Yasuda. But when their coffee arrived he pushed back his cuff once more.

'You need to get going, don't you? We'll make ourselves scarce,' said Yaeko, making to leave.

'Hmm . . .' Yasuda, puffing on a cigarette, narrowed his eyes as if to think. 'To be honest, I'll feel a little lonely if we part ways like this. How about you see me off at Tokyo station?' It was hard to tell from his expression whether he was joking or serious.

The two waitresses looked at each other. They were already late for work, and going to the station would only delay them further. But behind Yasuda's casual tone they detected a peculiar seriousness. Perhaps he really did feel lonely. And there was the fact that he had just treated them to a meal. No, it would hardly do for them to turn him down.

'Of course.' It was Tomiko who replied first, and decisively. 'I'll just phone the Koyuki and tell them we'll be a little late,' she said. She returned shortly afterwards, a smile on her face. 'That's all sorted. Now, let's see you off.'

'Sorry to put you out like this,' said Yasuda as he rose from his seat. He glanced at his wrist once again. The man certainly looks at his watch a lot, thought the waitresses.

'Which train are you getting?' asked Yaeko.

'The 6.12, or the one after that. It's twenty-five to six now, so if we leave right away we'll be there in good time,' Yasuda said, hurrying off to pay the bill.

It was a five-minute taxi ride to the station. On the way, Yasuda apologized again.

'Oh, don't worry, Ya-san, it's the least we can do,' said Yaeko.

'Yes, it's really no bother!' added Tomiko.

When they arrived, Yasuda bought his ticket and gave the waitresses platform tickets. His train to Kamakura, on the Yokosuka line, left from platform 13. The electronic clock showed almost six o'clock.

'Ah, good. I'll catch the 6.12,' said Yasuda.

5

His train had not yet arrived at the platform. As they waited, Yasuda looked east towards tracks 14 and 15, from which the long-distance trains departed. One such train was currently waiting at platform 15. The tracks in between were clear, giving them an unobstructed view from where they were standing.

'That's the Asakaze Express. Goes all the way down to Hakata in Kyushu,' remarked Yasuda.

The platform was already buzzing with the excitement of an imminent departure. Passengers bustled about in front of the train, accompanied by those seeing them off.

It was then that Yasuda exclaimed: 'Look! Isn't that Toki?'

Yaeko and Tomiko, their eyes round with astonishment, turned to see where he was pointing.

'Oh, yes! That's her all right,' said Yaeko excitedly. And indeed it was Toki making her way through the crowd on platform 15. From her elegant outfit and the suitcase in her hand, it was clear she was about to board the train. Tomiko, finally spotting her, cried out: 'Goodness, it *is* her!'

3

The waitresses were even more startled to see Toki chatting away merrily to a young man at her side. They could only see the man in profile, but he didn't look familiar. He was wearing a dark overcoat and carrying a small suitcase. The pair kept appearing and disappearing as they threaded their way through the crowd on the platform, heading for the rear of the train.

'Where could they be going?' asked Yaeko, scarcely able to catch her breath.

'And who is *he*?' exclaimed Tomiko.

Unaware that she was being observed, Toki continued along the platform with her companion. After a while, they stopped in front of one of the carriages and appeared to check which number it was. Then, the man leading the way, they boarded the train and disappeared from view.

'Quite the dark horse, our Toki! Off to Kyushu with her boy-friend, you reckon?' said Yasuda, grinning to himself.

The two waitresses stood rooted to the spot, their faces still screwed up in surprise. They stared wordlessly at the carriage into which Toki had disappeared as passengers continued to mill around in front of the train.

'I wonder . . .' said Yaeko after a moment. 'Must be travelling a long way if they're taking an express.'

'So she had a boyfriend all this time?' asked Tomiko.

'Who would have thought it!'

Tomiko and Yaeko had both dropped their voices, as if they had discovered something extraordinary.

In fact, neither of them knew much about Toki's personal life. She had never been one to talk about herself. They knew she wasn't married, and they'd never heard about any lovers or flings. In general, women in their line of work were either entirely open with their colleagues and wanted to talk about everything or they wrapped themselves in silence. Toki was one of the silent ones. As a result, the two waitresses were shocked to have stumbled across this secret corner of her life.

'I'm going over there to see who he is,' said Yaeko eagerly.

'No, don't. We should leave them to it!' said Yasuda.

'Come on, Ya-san – aren't you jealous?'

Yasuda laughed. 'Why would I be? I'm off to see my wife!'

Soon the train for Kamakura pulled into platform 13, blocking their view of platform 15 entirely. It would later be known that this train had arrived at 6.01.

Yasuda boarded his train, waving goodbye to the waitresses as he climbed into the carriage. His train was due to leave in eleven min-utes, and he would have a short wait on his hands. He leaned out of the window and told the waitresses: 'I'll be all right from here, thank you. Shouldn't you be getting back?'

'I suppose we should,' said Yaeko, who was in fact dying to rush over to platform 15 and get a closer look at Toki's companion. 'Well, we'll be off then, Ya-san.'

'Goodbye. And see you soon!'

The two women shook his hand and took their leave. As they walked down the stairs from the platform, Yaeko turned to her friend.

'Tomi-chan, how about we go and take a look?'

'I'm not sure we should . . .' replied Tomiko, but her show of reluctance was less than convincing, and soon the two of them were running back up another flight of stairs that led to platform 15.

They found the right carriage and, standing among the crowd on the platform, peeked through the window. In the train's well-lit interior, Toki and her companion were easy to spot.

'Look at her, chattering away!' said Yaeko.

'He's pretty good-looking, too. How old do you reckon he is?' said Tomiko, clearly more interested in Toki's companion.

'Twenty-seven or so, I'd guess.' Yaeko narrowed her gaze. 'No, twenty-nine, maybe.'

'So a few years older than her.'

'Let's go and surprise her.'

'No, Yae-chan, don't!' Tomiko stopped her friend from climbing on to the train. Then they watched for a little longer, until Tomiko managed to drag Yaeko, who was still looking on enviously, away from the scene.

'Come on, let's go. We're late.'

Back at the Koyuki, they immediately told the proprietress what they had seen. She was just as startled as they'd been.

'Well I never! Yesterday, she asked me for five or six days off so she could visit her family home. She never said anything about a man!'

'I suppose that was just an excuse. Anyway, didn't she say she was from Akita, up north?'

'And she always seemed so well-behaved! Just goes to show – you can never tell with people. I bet they're strolling happily around Kyoto or somewhere by now . . .' The three women exchanged knowing looks.

The following evening, Yasuda returned to the Koyuki with another client. After seeing his guest off as usual, he turned to Yaeko. 'No Toki today, I assume?'

'Not just today. She's taken the whole week off!' replied Yaeko, her eyebrows raised.

'Has she now! Off on their honeymoon then, you reckon?' said Yasuda, sipping his drink.

'I suppose so. I just can't believe it!'

'What's so hard to believe? If anything, you girls should follow her lead!'

'No such luck for us. Unless *you* fancied whisking us away, Ya-san?'

'Ha, me? No chance. I couldn't handle the lot of you.'

After chatting a little longer, Yasuda left the restaurant. He was back again the next evening with another two clients. Again Yaeko and Tomiko waited on him, and again their conversation turned to Toki.

But it wasn't long before Toki and her companion were found dead – and in a rather unlikely location.

2. Double Suicide

I

Three stops before Hakata, coming from Moji on the Kagoshima main line, there is a small station named Kashii. From there, the road to the mountains leads to a former imperial shrine. Head across the sea, however, and you reach a shore that looks out across Hakata bay. It is a beautiful view: in front, a thin spit of land known as Umi-no-Nakamichi girdles the bay, the half-island of Shikanoshima rising from the sea at its farthest reach, while off to the left the hazy outline of Nokonoshima island is faintly visible.

This section of shore, these days known simply as Kashii beach, was once referred to as the 'tidelands of Kashii'. In the eighth century, the governor Ōtomo no Tabito, passing by, composed a celebrated poem:

Come all – on the tidelands of Kashii,
Let us gather seaweed for breakfast,
Our white sleeves grazing the water.

But the harsh present has no time for such lyricism. At around six thirty on the cold morning of the twenty-first of January, a labourer was making his way along the shore. Instead of gathering seaweed for breakfast, he was heading to a factory in Najima.

It was barely dawn. A milky haze lay over the bay, through which Umi-no-Nakamichi and Shikanoshima dimly emerged. The cold wind was laced with brine. The labourer had turned up the collar of his coat and walked briskly, his body hunched. This rugged beach was the fastest route to the factory, and he walked along it every day.

But today that routine was broken. With his gaze cast downwards, he couldn't miss them. Two bodies were lying on the dark rocks, an unwelcome blight on this familiar landscape.

They were stretched out bleakly in the pale half-light of morning. The hems of their clothing flapped in the cold wind but, other than their hair, nothing moved. Their black shoes and white tabi socks remained motionless. Bewildered, the labourer broke into a run, diverting from his usual route and racing all the way to town, where he rapped on the window of a small police station.

'There are bodies on the beach!'

'Bodies?' The elderly policeman, who had just woken up, buttoned his coat against the cold as he listened to this breathless visitor.

'Yes, sir. Two of them. A man and a woman.'

'Where are they?' The policeman's eyes had opened wide at the sudden turn his morning had taken.

'Not far from here. On the beach. I'll show you.'

'Right. Just wait a moment.'

Although shaken, he had the presence of mind to write down the labourer's name and address and make a phone call to the main Kashii police station. Then the two of them set off in a hurry. Their breath hung white in the icy air.

When they reached the beach, the bodies were still lying there, exposed to the sea wind. With the policeman now at his side, the labourer could observe the bodies more calmly.

It was the woman who drew his attention first. She lay on her back, facing upwards. Her eyes were closed, but her open mouth revealed a set of bright white teeth. Her face was an almost rosy pink. Beneath a dark grey winter coat she wore a maroon silk kimono, its white collar slightly loose at the neck. Her clothes were immaculate. Lying there gracefully, she seemed to be merely sleeping. The hem of her kimono fluttered in the wind, revealing its yellow lining. On her primly aligned feet were a pair of pristine white tabi socks. There was no trace of dirt on them. Immediately next to her, also neatly arranged, was a pair of plastic zori sandals.

Now the labourer turned his gaze to the man. His face was tilted to the side. He, too, had the rosy cheeks of the living and resembled nothing so much as a drunk who had simply dozed off. From under his dark blue overcoat extended a pair of brown trousers, and his feet, in a pair of black shoes, were almost casually outstretched. The shoes were well polished and had clearly been looked after; his socks were navy blue, with red stripes.

The two bodies lay very close to each other. A small crab had clambered out of a crack in the rocks and was trying to crawl into an empty orange-juice bottle lying near the man.

'Double suicide, looks like . . .' said the elderly policeman, looking down at them.

'The poor things. Still so young, too.'

The beach was beginning to take on the colour of day.

2

Around forty minutes later, having received a call from Kashii police station, a chief detective, two other detectives, the police doctor and a forensics expert all arrived from Fukuoka by car. When they had taken photos of the bodies from various angles, the doctor squatted next to them to get a closer look.

'Potassium cyanide, the pair of them,' he said. 'These rosy cheeks of theirs are a dead giveaway. They must have taken it with the orange juice.'

The dregs of an orange liquid could be seen in the juice bottle that lay on the ground.

'How long have they been dead, Doctor?' asked the chief detective, who had a small moustache.

'We won't know for sure until we take them in, but I'd say ten hours or so.'

'Ten hours . . .' muttered the chief detective, casting his gaze around the scene. That would mean around ten or eleven the previous night. His eyes darted about, as if imagining how the double suicide might have played out.

'And they took the cyanide at the same time?'

'That's right. Must have mixed it with the juice.'

'Bit of a cold place to choose to die,' said someone in a low voice, almost a murmur, as if addressing no one in particular. The doctor, turning to see who it was, found a thin, unimposing man in a battered overcoat. He must have been in his late forties.

'Ah, Torigai,' said the doctor, after taking in the detective's creased features. 'Well, I'd say that's something only the living would worry about. Temperature doesn't make much difference to the dead. Come to think of it, orange juice isn't exactly a winter drink either. Yes . . .' He chuckled to himself. 'They must have been in quite the deviant state of mind. Rather than thinking rationally, I suppose they succumbed to a sort of perverse ecstasy.'

Now it was the detectives who chuckled among themselves, amused by the doctor's overblown rhetoric.

'Not to mention the fact that drinking poison takes a certain kind of resolve,' the chief detective observed. 'Yes, I suppose they'd have to be a little disturbed to go through with a thing like this.'

'Chief, any chance this could be a murder-suicide?' asked one of the other detectives, speaking in a broad Hakata accent.

'No. Clothes are undisturbed, no signs of a struggle . . . I'd say it's clear they took the cyanide by mutual consent.'

It was true. The woman's body lay there peacefully on the ground. Her white socks looked as though they had been removed only moments ago from the sandals arranged neatly next to her. Her hands were clasped together.

Now that it was clear they were dealing with a double suicide, the expressions on the detectives' faces relaxed. Indeed, with no crime having been committed, and no culprit for them to investigate, they seemed at something of a loose end.

The two bodies were taken in a van to the station. The detectives, shrugging and shivering against the cold, climbed into their car too. And, relieved of their unusual presence, the windswept bay of Kashii, lit by the pale sunlight of the winter morning, became tranquil once more.

Back at the station, the bodies were thoroughly examined. Photos were taken as their clothing was removed, one layer at a time. It was a painstaking operation.

A small wallet fell out of the man's jacket pocket, and from it they learned his identity. It contained a commuter pass, valid between Asagaya and Tokyo, in the name of Kenichi Sayama, thirty-one years old. The business cards provided further details. Next to his name was his position: 'Assistant Section Chief, Section X, Ministry X'. On the left was his home address.

The detectives exchanged glances. The section of the ministry in question was currently embroiled in a bribery scandal. Newspaper articles were appearing on the subject almost every day.

'No suicide note?' asked the chief.

They searched thoroughly but found nothing resembling one in any of his pockets. Just shy of ten thousand yen in cash, a hand-kerchief, a shoehorn, a folded copy of the previous day's newspaper and a crumpled receipt from a train dining car.

'A dining-car receipt? Odd thing for him to be carrying about.'

The chief took the receipt and carefully smoothed it out. It had apparently been forgotten in the man's pocket and was in a fairly battered state.

'Dated the fourteenth of January,' read the chief. 'Train number 7. One person. Total of three hundred and forty yen. Issued by the Japan Dining Company. Doesn't say what he ordered.'

3

'Do we know who the woman is?' asked one of the detectives.

Soon they did. Loose in her folding purse, along with around eight thousand yen, were four or five small business cards.

'*Toki – Koyuki Restaurant – Akasaka, Tokyo*' read the flowing script on the cards.

'Toki must be her name. Looks like she was a waitress at the Koyuki in Akasaka,' concluded the chief detective. 'So, the love suicide of a government official and a restaurant waitress. Plausible enough, I'd say.' He ordered telegrams to be sent to the addresses on the cards.

The bodies were examined in greater detail by the police doctor.

No external wounds were found. In both cases, the cause of death was cyanide poisoning, with the time of death estimated at between nine and eleven o'clock the previous evening.

'So they went for a walk on the beach, then committed suicide together,' remarked a detective.

'I imagine they . . . savoured their last moments with each other,' added another. But the doctor informed them that the bodies bore no signs of sexual relations prior to death. The detectives looked somewhat surprised to hear this; one of them remarked that they had died 'rather innocently'. It was again confirmed that the deaths were caused by cyanide poisoning.

'Seems they left Tokyo on the fourteenth,' said the chief, looking at the date on the dining-car receipt. 'Today's the twenty-first, so they set off a week ago. I imagine they stopped off somewhere along the way, then came to Fukuoka and decided on a place to die. Go and ask the station which train this number 7 is, will you?'

One of the detectives went to make the phone call and soon returned to report: 'Apparently it's a super-express from Tokyo to Hakata. The Asakaze.'

'A super-express to Hakata?' said the chief, cocking his head. 'That suggests they travelled straight here from Tokyo. In which case they spent the week in Fukuoka, or at least somewhere in Kyushu. Either way, they will have had luggage, and we need to find it. Take their photos and ask around the inns in town,' he ordered the detectives.

'Chief,' said one of the detectives, stepping forward. 'Could I see that receipt a moment?'

It was the thin, dark-skinned man with large eyes who had been at Kashii beach. His overcoat was as battered as the clothes beneath it, his face unshaven, and his tie twisted and worn. His name was Jūtarō Torigai, and he was one of the veterans of Fukuoka Police.

Torigai unfolded the receipt with his thin and not particularly clean fingers and inspected it.

'One person, it says. So he ate alone in the dining car,' he muttered, as if to himself.

'Well, yes,' interjected the chief detective in a sceptical tone. 'I imagine she didn't feel like eating, so he went on his own.'

'But . . .' murmured Torigai.

'But what?'

'Well, Chief, it's just . . . women, you know, they enjoy their food. And even if they're not hungry, they'll often get a little something just so they can keep their partner company. You know – a dessert, coffee, that kind of thing.'

The chief laughed. 'You might have a point. But maybe this particular woman was so full she couldn't even manage that.'

Torigai seemed to want to add something, then changed his mind. He put on his hat. With its crooked brim, it had clearly seen better days. Wearing it, he cut an even more unusual figure. He left the room, dragging the worn heels of his shoes across the floor.

With most of the detectives gone, the room felt oddly empty. Only one or two younger detectives remained, tending to the charcoal burner and occasionally refilling the chief's teacup.

The afternoon passed in this quiet manner. But, just as the sunlight coming through the windows was beginning to dwindle, there was a sudden flurry of footsteps down the corridor and a gaggle of people poured into the room. These were not the returning detectives but newspaper reporters.

'Chief!' cried one of the reporters. 'We've just heard from our head office in Tokyo that a Mr Sayama, assistant section chief at Ministry X, has died in a love suicide pact. We ran right over here!' It seemed the Tokyo newspapers had got wind of the telegram sent from the station that morning and issued an urgent dispatch to their Fukuoka bureaus.

4

The next day, the story of the love suicide of Kenichi Sayama, assistant section chief at Ministry X, was splashed across the morning newspapers. In addition to the two biggest dailies in Japan, which were printed in the nearby cities of Kokura and Moji, the most prominent local newspapers also devoted large front-page columns to the incident.

This was no ordinary double suicide. The deaths were being linked with the ongoing bribery investigation at the ministry. All the newspapers assumed that Sayama's death was in some way related to the scandal. They reported the official line from the public prosecutor in Tokyo that there had been no plans to summon Sayama as a witness. But various opinion pieces suggested that, knowing he would eventually be hauled in for questioning, he had committed suicide in a bid to prevent the scandal from reaching the upper ranks of the ministry.

These newspapers were piled on a corner of the chief's desk, but the chief was busy inspecting the contents of a small leather suitcase.

The suitcase had been discovered by one of the detectives, who, late into the previous night, had made the rounds of all the inns within Fukuoka city limits. The young detective in question had retrieved it from an inn called Tambaya, whose staff had confirmed that the man in the photo had indeed been a recent guest. The corresponding entry in the inn's register read: 'Taizo Sugawara, 32, office worker, 26 Minami Nakadori, Fujisawa City'. He had stayed there alone from the evening of the fifteenth until the night of the twentieth, when he had departed after settling his bill. On leaving, he had asked the inn to keep the case, saying he would be back for it later.

The suitcase contained various unremarkable items – toiletries, changes of shirts and underwear and a couple of magazines the man had probably bought on the train. There wasn't even a notebook, let alone a suicide letter.

When the chief had finished looking through the suitcase, he turned to the young detective who had brought him this useful piece of evidence.

'Did you say he stayed alone at the inn?' he asked.

'Yes, that's what they told me.'

'Hmm . . . odd. I wonder what the woman was up to then. Where could she have been all that time? The evening of the fifteenth is when they arrived at Hakata on the Asakaze. So he stayed alone at the inn until the night of the twentieth?'

'Yes. They said he didn't go out even once.'

'And the woman didn't drop by to see him at all?'

'No. He didn't have any visitors.'

While the chief was asking his questions Jūtarō Torigai grabbed his old hat and slipped quietly from the room.

Outside, he boarded a tram. He gazed absent-mindedly at the scenery passing by the window until, a short while later, he reached his stop. His unhurried movements were like those of an old man.

He made his way down a series of streets, still walking at a leisurely pace. Eventually, he found himself slowly looking up to find a building whose sign read 'Tambaya'. From the entrance he could see a well-polished corridor leading inside.

A clerk emerged and, seeing Torigai's police ID, straightened up respectfully.

Torigai confirmed the details the young detective had reported to the chief. Then, his rugged cheeks wrinkling with a smile, he asked, 'How did he seem to you when he got here?'

'He was very tired. Went to bed straight after his dinner,' replied the clerk.

'Can't have been much fun staying in all day. How did he pass the time?'

'Well, he mainly sat around reading and dozing. He didn't call the maid much. According to her, he was rather a gloomy sort. Seemed to be waiting for a phone call, as if it might come at any moment.'

'A phone call?' Torigai raised an eyebrow.

'Yes. He told us he was expecting one. Asked us to put it through as soon as it came. I assumed that was why he stayed in the whole time.'

'That does sound possible,' nodded Torigai. 'And did the phone call come?'

'Yes. I answered it myself. It was on the twentieth, around eight in the evening. A woman, asking to speak to Mr Sugawara.'

'A woman, you say . . . And she asked for Mr Sugawara, not Mr Sayama?'

'That's right. I knew he'd been waiting for the call the whole time, so I put her through straight away. We have a switchboard, and phones in all the rooms, you see.'

'I don't suppose you overheard the conversation?'

The clerk chuckled. 'We're not in the habit of listening in on our guests' phone calls.'

Torigai gave a quiet sigh of disappointment. 'What happened after that?'

'The call must have lasted about a minute. As soon as it was finished, he sent for his bill, paid it and walked out, leaving his suitcase with us. I never would have dreamed he was off to commit suicide . . .'

Torigai rubbed his unshaven chin with one hand as he sifted through his thoughts.

After arriving on the fifteenth, Assistant Section Chief Sayama had done nothing but wait impatiently at the inn for this phone call from a woman. Then, when the call finally came, he had left immediately, and committed suicide later that very evening. It was quite a strange sequence of events.

Torigai still couldn't shake the image of that dining-car receipt for 'one person' from his mind. Sayama had been waiting at the inn for his suicide partner to arrive – but why on earth did he have to wait five whole days?

3. The Two Stations in Kashii

I

It was around seven o'clock when Jūtarō Torigai got home. The front door clattered as he opened it, but nobody came out to greet him. As he was taking off his shoes in the narrow entrance, he heard his wife's voice from the other side of the inner door.

'Evening! Your bath's ready.'

By this she meant she wanted him to take his bath before dinner. He slid the door open and found her clearing away her knitting. A white cloth had been draped over the dining table.

'I thought you might be home late, so Sumiko and I have already eaten. She's out at the cinema with Nitta. Anyway, your bath's waiting.'

Torigai quietly undressed. His suit was worn, its lining frayed. Dust and sand had gathered in the cuffs of his trousers, and now fell with a patter here and there on the tatami. It was as though he were shedding all the exhaustion of his long day walking on to the floor.

His work meant he came home at irregular times. If he wasn't back by half past six, his wife and daughter would usually eat without him. Sumiko was his daughter, and Nitta her fiancé.

Torigai, still silent, climbed into the tub. The bath was in the old Goemon style, a metal cauldron heated directly from below.

'Is the water okay?' asked his wife.

'Yes, fine,' he replied, in a weary tone that suggested he wasn't in the mood for talking. He liked to lose himself in his own thoughts when he was in the bath.

He thought about the previous night's double suicide. What

could have driven the young couple to take their own lives? Their relatives in Tokyo had sent telegrams saying they would come to claim the bodies, so perhaps he would soon find out. The newspapers had latched on to the idea that Sayama had been heavily implicated in the ongoing corruption scandal at Ministry X, and that his suicide would have come as a relief to certain high-ranking officials. They reported that Sayama had been a dutiful but timid man. The papers also claimed that he and Toki had been deeply involved, and that he had previously hinted at his concern about where the relationship might lead. So had Sayama simply seen suicide as a way of solving his two problems – the ministry scandal and the relationship – in one stroke? No, it was more likely that his anxiety over the scandal had been his main motivation, and that the situation with Toki had simply propelled him even more quickly towards suicide.

Still . . . Torigai splashed his face with hot water. They had arrived together at Hakata station on the Asakaze, but where had the woman gone after leaving Sayama alone at the inn? Sayama had turned up at the inn on the evening of the fifteenth. According to the dining-car receipt in his pocket, that had also been the day of his arrival in Hakata, so he must have gone straight there. By that point the woman was no longer with him. For five days, from the sixteenth to the twentieth, Sayama had waited impatiently at the inn to hear from her. Where had Toki gone in the meantime, and what had she done?

Torigai wiped his face with a towel.

The phone call must have been important to Sayama, or he wouldn't have holed up at the inn like that. The woman had finally called at eight o'clock on the evening of the twentieth. It must have been Toki, because she asked for Sugawara rather than Sayama. The two of them had clearly agreed on the fake name in advance. Then, after the phone call, Sayama had left immediately, as if that had been his cue. That night, they had committed suicide on Kashii beach. This seemed a little hasty of them. Surely, now that they were finally reunited, they could have enjoyed each other's company a little first?

Torigai climbed out of the tub. However, instead of lathering himself with soap as usual, he simply sat with his thoughts as his body cooled.

Had certain urgent circumstances forced them to cut short their last moments together? If so, what were they? There had been no suicide note, but that didn't have to mean anything. Generally, only the very young tended to write them. Those who didn't were often acting under pressure. Presumably Sayama hadn't had the presence of mind to write one, and Toki had followed his example. It had been that kind of love suicide. Yes, there was no doubting it: this was a love suicide, all right. And yet . . .

Realizing he had become chilly, Torigai eased himself back into the bath.

And yet something about that dining-car receipt 'for one' bothered him. Maybe he was attaching too much importance to it, but . . .

'Been in there quite a while, haven't you?' his wife called to him.

2

Torigai made his way to the dining table, his face still flushed from the bath. He liked to spend his evenings savouring a bottle of sake. Small dishes of sea urchin, squid sashimi and dried cod strips were laid out on the table. He was tired from the day's walking, and the sake tasted delicious.

His wife was sewing a kimono now. With its lively red pattern, it was clearly intended for their soon-to-wed daughter. His wife seemed absorbed in the needle's movements.

'Rice,' he said, setting down his sake cup.

She set aside her needle and served him a bowl of rice, before immediately returning to the kimono. She carried on sewing while waiting to serve him again.

'How about joining me, even just for a cup of tea?'

'No, I'm fine, thank you,' she replied, without looking up. Torigai contemplated her as he tucked into his rice. She had grown old, just like he had. Clearly, at that age, the idea of keeping him company while he ate was no longer appealing. He munched on a pickled vegetable, then took a sip of his green tea.

Just then, his daughter came home. Her face was glowing; clearly she was in good spirits.

'Where's Nitta?' asked his wife.

'He saw me home, then headed back to his place,' replied Sumiko merrily. She took off her coat and sat down.

Setting aside his newspaper, Torigai turned to his daughter. 'Sumiko, tell me, on the way back from the cinema, did the two of you drop in somewhere for a cup of tea?'

She burst out laughing. 'Where did *that* come from? Yes, as a matter of fact, we did.'

'I see. In that case,' Torigai continued, moving on to the question that had been on his mind, 'imagine Nitta's hungry and he wants to get some food. But you're really not hungry – you couldn't even stomach a bite . . .'

'What funny ideas you're having!'

'Just listen a moment, will you? Suppose Nitta then said: "I'll eat something on my own, and you can go window shopping until I'm done." Would you do as he suggested?'

'Hmm . . .' she began, pensively. 'I think I'd want to go with him to the restaurant. It'd be better than just waiting around on my own.'

'Of course. What if you didn't even feel like a cup of tea?'

'Even then, I'd still want to sit with him. If I really couldn't eat, I'd order a coffee or something, just to keep him company.'

'As I thought,' he said, nodding. His tone was so serious that his wife, who had been sewing away silently, began to laugh.

'What on earth are you asking all this for?'

'Oh, shush!' he snapped, still smarting from her refusal to keep him company while he ate. Turning to his daughter, he continued: 'And . . . that's because you'd feel bad for Nitta otherwise?'

'Yes. You might say it's a question of affection more than appetite.'

'Ah, I see.' She's hit the nail on the head there, he thought. His daughter had distilled all his thoughts into one sentence. *A question of affection more than appetite* – yes, that had to be it.

Torigai had become fixated on that dining-car receipt for 'one person' because it was the point at which his vague but nagging doubts about the case seemed to converge. Sayama and Toki had been setting out on their final journey, to distant Kyushu, where they were to commit suicide. They would have been feeling even more affection for each other than usual. And they were on a train together. Even if Toki hadn't been hungry, surely it would have been natural for her to accompany her lover to the dining car, even just for a cup of coffee? They had reserved seats, so there was no risk of losing them. Had she perhaps stayed behind to watch their luggage? No, that didn't seem likely either. Torigai couldn't shake the feeling that there was something off about Sayama and Toki's relationship.

Their behaviour in Hakata had been strange, too. Toki had left Sayama at the inn for five days and gone off somewhere on her own. On the fifth evening she had telephoned him, and shortly afterwards they had ended their lives. There was something about Toki's behaviour that didn't seem to fit the usual pattern of a love suicide.

But the two bodies lying side by side on the beach at Kashii had clearly been the result of just such a suicide. He had inspected the scene himself. There could be no mistake.

Perhaps I really am letting my imagination get the better of me, thought Torigai. But still he frowned as he puffed on his cigarette.

3

The next day, the victims' relatives arrived from Tokyo. They had come to claim the bodies, which had been kept in the hospital morgue after the autopsies had been carried out.

In Sayama's case, it was his older brother who turned up. He was a stout, distinguished-looking man with a moustache who must have been in his early forties. The business card he handed over revealed him to be the manager of a bank branch.

As for Toki, an old woman of around sixty announced herself as her mother. She was accompanied by an elegantly dressed young woman, probably twenty-seven or twenty-eight years old. The young woman identified herself as Tomiko, one of the waitresses at the Koyuki restaurant in Akasaka where Toki had worked.

Strangely enough, the two parties who had come to claim the bodies ignored each other completely. Though obliged to spend much of the day together, whether at the investigation room at the police station or in the waiting room at the hospital, each studiously avoided the other. In fact, the awkward atmosphere seemed to emanate from Sayama's brother, the bank manager, who glared at the women with evident distaste, never relaxing his stiff expression, as if seeking to convey just how reprehensible he found them. The two women were left in a rather helpless position; they seemed intimidated by him and practically cowered under his gaze. This tension became particularly apparent when the chief questioned each of them in turn.

'Do you know of any circumstances that might have led your brother to commit suicide with this woman?' he asked.

The bank manager launched into a slightly pompous response.

'I'm afraid my brother has been a great embarrassment to us. The newspapers have been suggesting all sorts of reasons for his suicide, but to be honest I haven't the faintest idea what goes on at these government ministries. Of course, I wouldn't be able to tell you whether his suicide was really an attempt to protect his superiors. When I last saw him, maybe three weeks ago, he did seem quite despondent, but he didn't mention any details. He was never talkative that way. He lost his wife three years ago and there had been talk of him remarrying. He never seemed very keen on the idea, though, and the plans had stalled. I didn't even know he had a mistress until all this happened. My brother was quite a serious sort, you see. A close friend of his, whom I met just before I left Tokyo, told me he'd been concerned about his relationship with this woman. I wish the idiot had come to me with his problems. The worst of it is that the woman in question was a waitress at an Akasaka restaurant. If it had been someone a little more respectable, I might find the whole thing easier to stomach! My brother wasn't

25

exactly experienced with women, and he must have been putty in the hands of a seasoned flirt like her. I'm sure she talked him into the suicide. Yes, I'll bet she had some thorny problem of her own that only death could resolve and decided to take him along for the ride. He had such a bright future ahead of him, and to think that he got mixed up with a woman like that instead . . . Really, it makes me sick!'

He seemed, by now, to be directing all his loathing for Toki towards the women who had come to claim her body. It wasn't just that he refused to talk to them; he seemed ready to hurl abuse at them, perhaps even to strike them, and might even have done so had there been nobody around and no need to maintain appearances.

Toki's mother, meanwhile, responded to the chief's questions as follows:

'Her real name is Hideko Kuwayama. We're from the countryside in Akita, where we've been farmers for many generations. We married her off, but things didn't work out with her husband, and since they separated she's been working in Tokyo. I think she was employed at a few other places before the Koyuki, but she only wrote two or three times a year, and I knew nothing about her life. I have five other children, you see, so while I did worry about her, I couldn't get worked up about every little thing. I rushed here as soon as I saw the telegram from the Koyuki. Poor Hideko, doing a thing like this . . .'

The old woman did not say this all at once but spoke in faltering bursts. Her face seemed quite wrinkled for her age, and the edges of her tearful eyes were so red and swollen that she could almost have been suffering from an ailment.

Tomiko, the waitress from the Koyuki, had the following to say:

'Toki and I were close friends, which is why the proprietress asked me to come. Toki started at the restaurant three years ago. She was popular with all our customers, and always looked after them well in the private dining rooms. But I don't think any of them ever met up with her outside the restaurant. She was the sensible type, and didn't talk about herself much – even as her close friend, I never knew much about her private life. But I don't remember ever hearing any nasty gossip about her. This suicide took us completely by surprise. We've all been asking ourselves: when did she get so involved with someone? I'd never heard of this Sayama myself. His photo was in the newspapers, but since neither the proprietress nor any of us waitresses recognized him, I don't think he was ever a customer at the Koyuki. But Yaeko and I did see him with Toki, at Tokyo station. Oh – Yaeko is another waitress at the Koyuki. She's a friend of mine.'

'You saw them together? Could you tell me about that?' asked the chief.

'It was the evening of the fourteenth. We were with one of our regulars, Mr Yasuda. Yaeko and I were seeing him off at Tokyo station, when all of a sudden we spotted Toki and that man getting on a train. We were on platform 13, but the tracks were clear and we could see right across to platform 15. Mr Yasuda said, "Look! Isn't that Toki?" And there she was, walking along the platform with the man, and then they boarded the express to Kyushu. We were stunned. Toki, of all people, jumping on a train with a lover! It was all so unexpected. Anyway, we wanted to know more about this secret of hers, so after we'd seen Mr Yasuda off we dashed over to platform 15 and had a peek through the train window. She was just sitting there next to the man, chatting away happily. We really couldn't believe our eyes!'

'And you didn't speak to her?'

'No, it felt like it was their little secret. We decided not to intrude and left them to it. It was definitely the man in the newspaper photo – this Mr Sayama. When I think they were actually off to commit suicide! Toki had asked for time off work, so I suppose it must have all been planned in advance. She was such a nice girl. I just feel so sorry for her. I can't think what could have driven her to take her own life. Like I said, she didn't talk much about private matters, and I don't know the details of her situation. But the newspapers say Sayama was badly mixed up in that bribery scandal, so maybe she just went along with him out of sympathy.'

These were the statements made by the three people who came to claim the bodies. Also present, and listening carefully, was Jūtarō Torigai.

4

The bodies were returned to the relatives, who had them cremated in Fukuoka before taking the ashes back to Tokyo. Then, as the days went by, the love suicide at Kashii beach receded smoothly and quietly into the past.

Torigai had not been in a position to interfere with the case. There were, however, two things that bothered him. The first was the dining-car receipt for 'one person' – that question of affection versus appetite. The second was the fact that Toki had not stayed at the inn with Sayama: where could she have gone during those five days?

But neither of these was strong enough grounds to refute the theory of double suicide. The chief would never take him seriously. He himself knew that, objectively speaking, it was a pretty shaky foundation. And so, though not fully convinced, he had decided to hold his tongue and simply let things take their course. But it was one thing to stay quiet, and quite another to set his own mind at ease: if anything, his reticence only made his doubts grow. If he wanted to put the case behind him, he would need clear answers to his two questions.

It was just a love suicide, he tried to tell himself. No crime had been committed. So why did he feel so reluctant to move on? After all, there were new cases coming in all the time that demanded his attention. But Torigai knew he would only be satisfied once he had laid his doubts to rest.

Looks like I'll have to investigate this one on my own, without telling anyone, he thought to himself. Once he had reached this decision, he felt oddly relieved, as if a weight had been lifted from his shoulders.

After causing a minor stir in the papers, where it had been linked to the bribery scandal, the double suicide had disappeared smoothly from view. Too smoothly, perhaps. There had been none of the usual detective work, probably because the story of two lovers committing suicide offered such a neat solution to the case. It was as though there was a gaping hole where all the steps leading to that conclusion should have been.

Torigai decided to return to Kashii beach, where the bodies had been found, and take another look at the scene.

He got off the tram in Hakozaki and changed to a Nishitetsu train bound for Wajiro. The Nishitetsu line was a privately owned electric railway that was more convenient for reaching Kashii than the national line. It also ran closer to the coast.

From Nishitetsu Kashii station it was a ten-minute walk to the

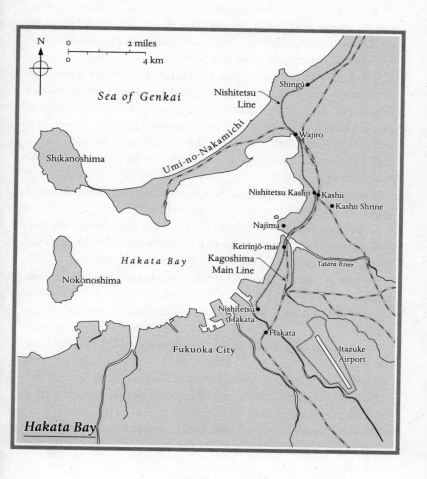

beach where the bodies had been found. A few dreary-looking houses stood on either side of the road, before abruptly giving way to a pine forest, which in turn yielded to the pebbled expanse of the beach. This area had once been part of the sea; it was all reclaimed land.

The wind was still cold, but now the sea had a bluish tinge that hinted at the coming of spring. The harsh, cold colours of winter had disappeared. A thin mist hung over the end of the peninsula.

Torigai stood at the scene of the double suicide. It was a dark, rocky spot with few distinguishing features, and he barely recognized it from that day in January. Here, even the most brutal of scuffles would have left no trace. Compared to the surrounding landscape, it was a rather desolate place.

Torigai wondered why Sayama and Toki had chosen a location like this in which to die. Surely they could have found a more appropriate spot. Usually, in cases like this, the lovers would opt for a suitably indulgent location – a hot-spring resort, say, or a well-known beauty spot – in which to end their lives. True, the view here wasn't bad, but they could at least have chosen a patch of soft grass over these unforgiving rocks.

But then he remembered that the suicide had taken place at night. They had left the inn at around eight in the evening and were dead by around ten. They had come straight here, as if they had planned it that way from the start. It had been a dark night – and yet they had acted as if they were already familiar with the area.

In which case . . . It occurred to Torigai that Sayama or Toki might have visited the area previously and got to know the lie of the land. Without such prior knowledge, their behaviour was hard to explain.

Torigai turned back the way he had come, upping his pace now. He passed Nishitetsu Kashii station and this time headed towards the mainline station instead. The two stations stood around five hundred metres apart, and the road connecting them ran through a busy neighbourhood.

At the station, he went to the telegraph office and, taking a battered notebook from his pocket, checked the addresses he had scribbled down. Then he dispatched two telegrams, one to Sayama's brother and the other to Toki's mother. It took some effort to fit what he wanted to say into the twenty-character limit.

This done, he went inside the station itself and looked up at the timetable. There was a train back to Hakata in around twenty minutes.

While he waited, he stood in the entrance of the station, his hands in his pockets, and looked out at the street. A dreary, unchanging scene greeted him. There was a small restaurant, a general shop, and another selling fruit. A truck had parked in the station forecourt, where two or three children were playing. The street was bathed in sunshine.

As Torigai gazed vacantly across the forecourt, a doubt crept into his mind. So far, he had assumed that Sayama and Toki had come to Kashii on the private Nishitetsu line. Wasn't it possible, though, that they had instead arrived here, at the mainline station? Looking at the timetable again, he saw that there was a train from Hakata that arrived at 9.24 in the evening.

Torigai closed his eyes to think for a moment. Then, instead of boarding his train back to Hakata, he made his way towards the shops on the other side of the forecourt. Torigai had some questions to ask. His pulse quickened with anticipation.

4. The Man from Tokyo

Torigai was standing in front of the fruit shop at Kashii station.

'Can I ask you something?'

The shopkeeper, a man of about forty who was busy polishing an apple, turned to look at him. Shopkeepers weren't always the most helpful people when questioned in this way, but when Torigai added that he was with the police, the man became more attentive.

'How late do you stay open in the evening?' asked Torigai.

'I close around eleven.'

'In that case, would you be able to see the passengers when they come out of the station at around nine thirty?'

'Nine thirty? Definitely. There's a train that gets in from Hakata at twenty-five past. The shop isn't very busy at that time of night, so I keep a lookout for potential customers.'

'I see. Then I wonder if, around that time on the evening of the twentieth of January, you might have spotted a man of around thirty, wearing Western clothes, and a woman of around twenty-five in a kimono and winter coat?'

'The twentieth, you say? Hmm . . .'

The shopkeeper nodded thoughtfully, but Torigai realized that the question might be difficult to answer. The twentieth was quite some time ago, and the shopkeeper probably wouldn't remember the exact date. He decided to change tack.

'Did you hear about that double suicide on the beach near here?'

'You mean the bodies they found that morning? Yes. People talked about them. It was in the papers, too.'

'That's right. They found them on the morning of the twenty-first, so the twentieth would have been the night before. Ringing any bells?'

'Ah!' The shopkeeper slapped his thigh through the thick apron he was wearing, which was printed with the shop's name. 'If it was the night before, then yes. I did see a couple like that.'

'You did?' Torigai's eyes lit up.

'That's right. I remember because the next day there was all the fuss about the bodies on the beach. There were only ten or so people on the nine twenty-five that evening. That train is never that busy, you see. And among them was a couple just like you described, a man in Western clothes and a woman in a kimono. I thought they might be the type to buy some fruit, so I kept a pretty close eye on them.'

'And did they buy anything?'

'No, they just hurried past and disappeared down the road towards the Nishitetsu station. I was a bit disappointed. And then, the next morning, there was all that commotion about the double suicide! I did wonder if it could have been them.'

'Do you remember their faces?'

Torigai looked intently at the shopkeeper, who was rubbing his chin as he tried to think.

'Well, they were pretty far away, so they were just these two dark figures against the bright lights of the station. I couldn't really make out their faces. The newspaper had a photo of the man who committed suicide, but I couldn't be sure it was the same person.'

'I see,' said Torigai, his shoulders drooping slightly. 'What about their clothes?'

'I don't really remember those either. I just saw them walking off in that direction, and the only thing I can recall is that the man was wearing an overcoat and the woman a kimono.'

'You weren't able to make out the kimono's pattern?'

'Not at all, I'm afraid!' replied the shopkeeper with an apologetic smile. Torigai felt a little discouraged.

A customer was in the shop, looking at the oranges. He seemed to be listening in on their conversation.

'When you say they were walking towards the Nishitetsu station – that's the same direction as the beach, isn't it?' asked Torigai.

'That's right. That road takes you all the way to the beach.'

Torigai thanked him and left the shop. This could all be useful information, he thought as he walked. His instincts had proved correct. Standing in front of the station, he had thought the fruit seller might have spotted something, and he had been right. It was a shame the shopkeeper hadn't seen their faces, but Torigai felt sure the pair in question had been Sayama and Toki. They had arrived that night on the 9.24 from Hakata. In that case, they would have boarded the train in Hakata at around 9.10.

It had been just after eight when Sayama received Toki's phone call and hurried out of the inn. In that case, where had the two met, and what had they done in the hour or so before boarding the train at Hakata? This would be difficult, if not impossible, to discover. In a city as big as Fukuoka, there would be simply no way of knowing where to start.

As Torigai walked towards the Nishitetsu station, lost in these thoughts, someone called out to him from behind.

'Excuse me!'

Torigai turned around and saw a young man who looked like he might be an office worker approaching with a bashful smile.

'Are you with the police?'

'I am.' Torigai saw that the man was holding a bag of oranges and realized that he was the customer who had been in the shop.

2

'I was buying some oranges and I couldn't help overhearing your conversation,' said the young man. 'That couple you were talking about – I saw them too, at around nine thirty on the night of the twentieth of January.'

'You saw them too?' Torigai's eyes widened. Looking around, he spotted what looked like a small café and invited the rather hesitant man to follow him there. Then, sipping a black, sugary liquid that he had been assured was coffee, he looked intently at the young man.

'Tell me what you saw.'

'Well, I'm not sure how much use this will be,' said the man, scratching his head. 'It's just that I overheard you talking in the shop and thought I should mention it, just in case.'

'I appreciate it. Please, go ahead.'

'I live around here, but I commute to an office in Hakata,' he began. 'On the night before they found the bodies – the night of the twentieth, that is – I also saw two people who might have been the couple from the suicide. They arrived at Nishitetsu Kashii station at 9.35.'

'Just a moment,' said Torigai, holding up a hand to interrupt. 'You mean they arrived on the Nishitetsu line, not the main line?'

'Yes, on the train that leaves Keirinjō-mae at 9.27. It gets here eight minutes later.'

Keirinjō-mae was in Hakozaki, east of Hakata. Hakozaki had been the site of an important battle during the Mongol invasion, and there were even remains of a fort dating from that era. Nearby flowed the Tatara river, and Hakata bay could be seen through the pine trees.

'I see. And did you see them on the train?'

'No, not on the train. The train had two carriages. I was in the rear one. There weren't many passengers, so if they'd been in my carriage I would have noticed them. They must have been in the front one.'

'So where did you see them?'

'I'd gone through the ticket gate and was walking home. I'd been drinking in Hakata and was a little tipsy, so I was walking quite slowly. A few passengers from my train had already overtaken me. They were all locals, and I knew them by sight. But there was also this couple I didn't recognize, walking past me at a brisk pace. The man was wearing an overcoat, and the woman a kimono beneath a winter coat. They headed off down the deserted road that leads to the beach. At the time, I paid no attention and turned down the side road that takes me home, but the next morning there was that incident at the beach. The papers said they died around ten o'clock that night, and that's when I realized it could well have been them.'

'Did you see their faces?'

'As I said, they overtook me and were walking quite quickly, so I only saw them from behind.'

'What about the colour of the man's coat, or the pattern on the woman's kimono?'

'I couldn't see that either. The lighting is pretty dim on this street and, like I said, I was a little tipsy. I did hear the woman say something, though.'

'You did?' Torigai's eyes gleamed. 'What did she say?'

'Just as they walked past, she said to the man: *What a lonely place.*'

'*What a lonely place . . .*' Torigai repeated in a murmur. 'And what did the man reply?'

'He didn't say anything. The two of them just kept on walking.'

'Was there anything distinctive about the woman's voice?'

'Well, I'd say it was pleasant-sounding. And she spoke in standard Japanese rather than the Hakata dialect. People round here don't talk like that. She sounded like she was from Tokyo.'

Torigai took a cigarette from a crumpled packet and lit it. The pale smoke drifted into the air while he thought about what to ask next.

'That train you were on – was it definitely the 9.35 into Nishitetsu Kashii?'

'Yes, I'm sure of it. Even when I'm out late drinking in Hakata, I always make sure to get that one home.'

Torigai paused and thought some more. What if the couple that had walked past this office worker were in fact the same couple the fruit seller had seen getting off at the mainline station? The office worker hadn't actually seen them on board the Nishitetsu train. He'd simply assumed they had been, because they overtook him just after he left the station. The mainline train arrived at 9.24, and the Nishitetsu train at 9.35 – a gap of eleven minutes. The two stations were about five hundred metres apart, and if you got off at the mainline station and headed towards the beach, the road took you past the Nishitetsu station. If it was the same couple, then both the route and the timing seemed to add up.

'Well, that's all I have to tell you,' said the good-natured office worker. As he made to leave, he looked at Torigai, who was still lost in his thoughts. 'I just thought I should mention it, seeing as I heard you asking questions in the shop.'

'Thank you very much,' said Torigai. He asked for the young

man's name and address, then gave a small bow in thanks. Just hearing about that remark by the woman was enough to leave him feeling that their conversation had been worthwhile.

By the time he left the café, it was completely dark.

3

What a lonely place.

The woman's words, as relayed by the office worker, echoed in Torigai's ears. It was as though he himself had overheard them. From this short phrase he deduced three things:

1. The woman spoke standard Japanese, so she couldn't have been a local. No one from Fukuoka, or even the wider Kyushu region, talked that way. In the local Hakata dialect, for example, the phrase would have sounded completely different.
2. What she said implied that this was her first time in the area.
3. Therefore, she had not been seeking the man's agreement but rather conveying her initial impression of the place, as if to someone who already knew it well. The fact that the man had not answered, instead pressing silently ahead, seemed to support this idea.

In short, the man had been to the area before, whereas it was the woman's first time. The woman had a Tokyo accent and had spoken these words shortly before the presumed time of their suicide – anything from thirty minutes to an hour and a half beforehand, depending on whether they had died closer to ten or eleven o'clock. It therefore seemed highly likely to Torigai that the fruit seller and the office worker had both spotted the couple who had committed suicide.

Of course, there was still reason to be cautious. Hakata alone would be home to several thousand people who were originally from Tokyo, and the fact that this couple had been walking near the beach that night might have been a complete coincidence, with no relation to the double suicide. But Torigai decided not to get too caught up in such thoughts. For now, he would assume they were indeed the suicidal lovers.

A cold wind was blowing, and the banners outside the shops fluttered forlornly. Stars glittered in sharp relief against the black sky.

Torigai made his way back to the mainline station. When he got there, he looked at his watch. It was old but kept good time.

He abruptly began walking, as if he had pushed the button on a timer. Hunched over with his hands in his pockets, he made his way briskly back towards the Nishitetsu station, his coat flapping in the wind.

When he reached the well-lit station, he checked his watch. It had taken him less than six minutes to get from the mainline station to this one.

Torigai thought for a moment. Then, glancing at his watch again, he set off back to the main station. This time, he slowed his pace slightly, judging his speed by the sound of his footsteps.

Back at the main station, he checked how long it had taken. Just over six minutes.

He set off once again. This time, he ambled along slowly, studying the houses on either side of the road as if out for a leisurely stroll. When he got to the Nishitetsu station, he saw that it had taken him around eight minutes.

From these three experiments, Torigai concluded that walking normally from the mainline station to the Nishitetsu station would take someone between six and seven minutes.

The couple the fruit seller had seen coming out of the mainline station had been on the 9.24. Meanwhile, the office worker had seen a couple walking from the Nishitetsu station, together with the passengers from the 9.35. An interval of eleven minutes. If these two sightings were indeed of one and the same couple, it had taken them eleven whole minutes to get from one station to the other.

What could this mean? It had taken them eleven minutes to walk a distance that, even walking at a very slow pace, had taken him only eight.

Then he remembered that the office worker had said they had walked past at a 'brisk pace'.

If they were walking that fast, it should have taken them barely five minutes. Two explanations for the eleven-minute gap seemed plausible to Torigai:

1. The couple had needed to stop on the way – to buy something, for example.
2. The fruit seller and the office worker had in fact spotted two separate couples.

Number one seemed plausible enough, while number two would render the discrepancy in timings irrelevant. Now that he thought about it, nothing proved that both sightings had been of the same couple. Their only common features were that the man wore an overcoat and the woman a kimono. No one had seen their faces or noticed the kimono's pattern.

In which case, thought Torigai, the pair spotted by the office worker near the Nishitetsu station must have been Sayama and Toki. The woman's remark was enough to convince him of this.

But he still couldn't be entirely sure that the couple seen at the mainline station were not the same two individuals. Theory number one seemed just as plausible. Torigai couldn't quite shake the idea that the two couples were the same.

In the end, he returned to his home in Hakata without reaching a satisfactory conclusion.

Two days later, when he came into the station in the morning, two telegrams were waiting on his desk.

The first read:

KENICHI OFTEN VISITED HAKATA ON BUSINESS

And the second:

HIDEKO HAD NEVER BEEN TO HAKATA

They were replies to the telegrams he had sent from Kashii station. The first was from Sayama's brother, the bank manager, while the second was from Toki's mother, Mrs Kuwayama.

It was just as he'd guessed: Sayama had been familiar with the area through his business trips, whereas Toki had come to Hakata for the first time.

A scene formed in Torigai's mind: the dark silhouette of a man, silently and briskly leading a woman to the beach, and the woman saying: *What a lonely place.*

4

That morning, Torigai finished some work at the office. Then he took a tram to Hakozaki and walked from there to Keirinjō-mae. The Nishitetsu line ran from this station all the way to the port of Tsuyazaki on the north coast, passing through Kashii along the way.

It was a sunny day, and unusually warm for winter. Torigai headed to the stationmaster's office, where he showed his police ID.

'What can I help you with?' asked the corpulent, ruddy-faced stationmaster from behind his desk.

'On the twentieth of January, a train on this line arrived at Kashii at 9.35 in the evening. What time would it have left here?' asked Torigai.

'Nine twenty-seven,' replied the stationmaster, without even pausing to think.

'I have something to ask the ticket inspector who was working at the gate that evening. Is he here now?'

'One moment.' The stationmaster asked his assistant to check the rota. The ticket inspector in question happened to be on duty, so the assistant went to fetch him.

'Is this for a case?' asked the stationmaster while they waited.

'Yes, something like that,' replied Torigai, taking a sip of the tea they had brought him.

'Must be hard work.'

A young station employee walked in, stood in front of the stationmaster and saluted.

'This is your man,' said the stationmaster.

'Sorry to bother you,' said Torigai, turning to the young man. 'You were checking tickets for the 9.27 on the twentieth, correct?'

'Yes, I was on duty.'

'Did you happen to see a man of around thirty wearing an overcoat, with a woman of around twenty-five in a kimono?'

'Hmm . . .' said the employee, blinking. 'There would have been plenty of men wearing coats. Do you know what colour it might have been?'

'A dark blue overcoat, and brown trousers. The woman would have been in a maroon kimono under a grey coat,' replied Torigai, describing the clothes found on the bodies at the beach. The station employee looked off into space, as if thinking hard.

'I'm sorry, I can't remember. We usually just look at the tickets when we're punching them – we don't see passengers' faces much, unless something out of the ordinary happens. Anyway, this is the first station on the line, so as soon as we open the ticket gates the passengers all pour on to the platform at once.'

'Still, I imagine there weren't too many of them at that time of day?'

'That's right. I'd say there were thirty or forty people here – around the same number as usual.'

'Lots of women wear Western clothes these days – you don't see many in kimonos any more. Doesn't that jog your memory at all?'

'I'm afraid it doesn't.'

'Please. Try to remember,' insisted Torigai.

But, after tilting his head to one side to think, the station employee repeated that he just couldn't recall. Then Torigai had another idea.

'Well, when you were checking tickets for that train, maybe there were some other passengers you did recognize?'

'Oh yes, there were a few.'

'I see. In that case, could you tell me their names?'

'Of course. There were three of them, if I remember correctly. I know them pretty well, so I can even tell you where they live.'

'That would be very helpful.'

Torigai took down the names and addresses, thanked the two men, and left the stationmaster's office. He had some legwork to do. The three addresses all lay along the Nishitetsu line. Torigai visited three stations in turn: Wajiro, Shingū and Fukuma.

The man in Wajiro told him the following:

'There were two carriages; I was in the front one. I remember two women in grey coats. One was around forty, and the other must have been twenty-six or twenty-seven. But the people sitting next to them were all young office girls. I don't remember any man in a dark blue coat.'

Torigai took a photo of Toki from his pocket and showed it to the man.

'The younger woman. Could this have been her?'

'No, that's not her. Her features were completely different.'

The man in Shingū said he'd boarded the train at the rear.

'A woman in a coat? I can't say I remember. I think there might well have been, but I fell asleep straight away. I certainly didn't see a man in a dark blue coat.' Torigai showed the man photographs of both Toki and Sayama, but he didn't recognize either of them.

The last of the three passengers, in Fukuma, said:

'I was sitting at the rear. There was a woman in a winter coat. Yes, she must have been twenty-five or twenty-six.'

'Was her coat grey?'

'I don't remember the colour, but winter coats often are, aren't they? Yes, I think it probably was. She was chatting away to the man sitting next to her.'

'A man? What did he look like?' asked Torigai with excitement, but the reply was disappointing.

'They appeared to be a couple, although he was quite a bit older – I would say in his forties. He was in a rather dishevelled kimono with Ōshima patterning.'

Again, Torigai took out the photos, but the man didn't recognize Toki or Sayama, nor could he remember any dark blue overcoat. In the end, having failed to unearth any solid evidence that Sayama and

Toki had been on the Nishitetsu train, Torigai returned to Hakata feeling dejected and exhausted.

When he arrived at the police station, the chief rose from his desk, as if he had been waiting for him. 'Torigai!' he called out. 'There's someone from the Tokyo Police here to see you.'

An unfamiliar young man in a suit was sitting next to the chief, a smile on his lips.

5. The First Doubt

I

The man who rose and greeted Torigai must have been just over thirty. He was not tall, but had a sturdy, almost box-like physique. Above his youthful, healthy-looking cheeks were a pair of thick eyebrows and two round eyes.

'Inspector Torigai? My name is Kiichi Mihara, inspector with the Second Investigative Division of the Tokyo Metropolitan Police. It's a pleasure.'

He smiled, revealing a set of pearly-white teeth, and handed Torigai his card.

Hearing the words 'Second Investigative Division', Torigai understood immediately that Mihara was here to investigate Kenichi Sayama's suicide. While the First Division dealt with violent offences, the Second handled what they call white-collar crime – cases of corruption or fraud.

By now, the Tokyo newspapers had begun to really dig their teeth into the bribery scandal at Ministry X. Kenichi Sayama's section lay at the heart of the affair. In fact, one of his colleagues, another assistant section chief, had already been arrested. Only a week ago, two senior managers at a major private organization with close links to the ministry had also been taken into custody. The case looked set to escalate further, and it was up to the Second Division to handle it.

'I'm here to clear a few things up in relation to the suicide of Kenichi Sayama, assistant section chief at Ministry X,' began Mihara, once he had settled back into his chair. It was just as Torigai had guessed.

'The chief here has just given me a rundown of the case,' he continued, glancing at the man at his side, who nodded. 'As you can see, I've been having a look at the evidence too. All very useful.' On the desk were the photographs taken at the scene of the suicide, together with the autopsy report and other case documents. 'But I'm informed, Inspector Torigai, that you had certain suspicions about this love suicide. Is that true?'

Torigai looked at the chief, who exhaled a cloud of cigarette smoke and said: 'You know – those observations you shared at the time. When I mentioned them to Inspector Mihara, he was very interested. Could you explain them to him?'

'That's right. The chief told me you had a rather different theory regarding Sayama's suicide and, I have to say, that piqued my curiosity. I've been waiting here to talk to you.' There was a friendliness in Mihara's large eyes. The chief, meanwhile, looked sceptical.

'Well, it's nothing as firm as a theory. Just a few thoughts, I suppose.' Torigai, conscious of his chief's presence, seemed hesitant.

But he had Mihara's attention now. 'A few thoughts are just what I'm after. Please, go ahead – I'm all ears.'

And so, a little reluctantly, Torigai explained about the dining-car receipt that had been issued for one person only. As he spoke, his daughter's comments about affection versus appetite came to mind, though he kept that part to himself.

'That certainly is an interesting observation,' nodded Mihara, a twinkle in his eyes. There was something in his cordial tone that reminded Torigai of an insurance salesman. 'You didn't keep the receipt?'

'Although their deaths were not from natural causes, there was no crime to speak of, so we returned all their private effects to the relatives who came for their bodies,' interjected the chief.

'I see.' A hint of disappointment flitted across Mihara's brow.

'The receipt was dated the fourteenth of January, correct?' he asked Torigai.

'That's right.'

'Which is the day Sayama and Toki set off from Tokyo on the Asakaze. Just a moment . . .' he began, pulling a notebook from his pocket. 'I've written the train timetable down here. It leaves Tokyo at

6.30 in the evening, then Atami at 8.00, Shizuoka at 9.01 and Nagoya at 11.21. After that, the next stop is Osaka, at 2 a.m. – which would be the following morning, the fifteenth of January. So, for a receipt dated the fourteenth, Nagoya would have been the last possible stop.'

Torigai began to grasp where Mihara was going with this. The inspector shared his suspicions about the case. He might come across like an insurance salesman, but he's Tokyo Police all right, thought Torigai.

Mihara turned to the chief.

'I'd like to visit the scene of the suicide. I know he's a busy man, but do you think I could borrow Inspector Torigai and have him show me the way?'

The chief reluctantly agreed.

2

On the tram, Mihara, clutching one of the hanging leather straps, said to Torigai in a low voice: 'Your boss didn't seem too happy, did he?'

Torigai gave a wry smile, creases appearing around his eyes.

'It's the same story everywhere you go,' continued Mihara. 'I wanted to hear more about your ideas, but I could see you were finding it hard to talk in front of him. That's why I asked you to show me to the beach.'

'I'll tell you all about it once we get there,' replied Torigai, impressed by young Mihara's thoughtfulness.

At Keirinjō-mae, they changed to a Nishitetsu train which took them to Kashii. From there it was less than ten minutes' walk to the scene of the suicide.

When they arrived at the beach, Mihara looked around with evident interest. It was a fine day, and the sea was an almost spring-like blue. A mist hung over the islands in the distance.

'So this is the famous Genkai sea. I glimpsed it from the train, but it's even more impressive up close,' said Mihara, gazing admiringly across the bay.

Torigai showed him the spot where the bodies had been found and explained how they had been lying. Mihara took the crime-scene photos from his pocket and compared them with what he could see, nodding away while Torigai spoke.

'Quite a rocky beach, isn't it?' said Mihara, looking around.

'Yes – as you can see, there are all these stones before you get to the sand.'

'So, no footprints . . .' murmured Mihara, as if contemplating something.

Once they had walked a little way from the scene of the suicide, and found a large rock to sit on, Mihara said, 'Well then, Inspector Torigai, care to tell me what's been on your mind?' The afternoon sun warmed their shoulders through their coats. Anyone passing by would have assumed they were simply out to enjoy the sunshine.

'The first thing is that dining-car receipt, for only one person,' began Torigai. He explained the reasoning behind his doubts, this time including his daughter's observation that this was a question of affection more than appetite. 'That's why I've come to suspect that Sayama was alone on that train.'

Mihara was listening attentively, his eyebrows raised. 'That is interesting. I actually had a similar feeling myself. But there are witnesses who saw him boarding the train with a woman at Tokyo station . . .'

'Exactly. Which might lead us to deduce that the woman – this Toki – got off somewhere along the way, don't you think?' said Torigai.

'It certainly might,' said Mihara, taking out his notebook. 'And the receipt is dated the fourteenth, so if she did get off the train, it must have been at Nagoya, at 11.21 p.m., or at one of the previous two stops. But the dining car closes at ten, so we can rule out Nagoya. In other words, if Toki left the train, it was either at Atami at 8.00, or at Shizuoka at 9.01.'

'Yes, that has to be it,' said Torigai, nodding pensively. Mihara was putting all his own vague suspicions into words.

'Right. It's been a while since all this happened, so I wouldn't hold your breath, but I'll make enquiries at Atami and Shizuoka stations and any nearby inns. You'd be surprised how well people tend to remember a woman travelling on her own.' Mihara went on: 'Is there anything else?'

'Sayama stayed alone at the Tambaya inn in Hakata from the fifteenth to the twentieth.' Torigai then explained how Sayama had waited in his room for a phone call; how at around eight o'clock on the night of the twentieth a woman had called, asking for him under the fake name of Sugawara; and how Sayama had then left his room immediately before committing suicide later that night.

Mihara had been listening intently. 'The caller knew Sayama's fake name, which means it was probably Toki,' he observed. 'The two of them must have agreed on the inn and the name in advance.'

'I think you're right. Well, that clears up one mystery.'

'Which is?'

'Previously, I'd assumed they'd arrived together in Hakata, and Toki had then disappeared somewhere. But if, as you say, she got off the train somewhere along the way, then she would have arrived later, wouldn't she? Toki must have disembarked at Atami or Shizuoka on the fourteenth, leaving Sayama to travel on alone, only arriving in Hakata on the twentieth. Then she called the inn. The fact that Sayama was waiting for that call implies they planned that part too. But,' continued Torigai, 'there was one thing they couldn't settle in advance.'

'What was that?'

'The exact timing of Toki's arrival in Hakata. Sayama sat there fretting at the inn, day after day, while he waited for her phone call. That suggests they'd been unable to set a specific date for her arrival.'

3

Mihara had been scribbling something in his notebook. When he had finished, he showed it to Torigai. 'I suppose it would look something like this.'

'Yes, that's it!' said Torigai, after studying the diagram.

'But then why did Toki get off the train along the way?' asked Mihara.

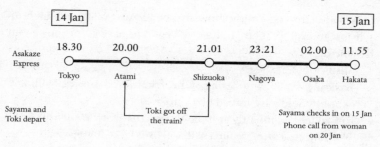

This was the question that Torigai had been unable to answer, no matter how much he racked his brains. 'That's what I just can't figure out,' he replied, putting a hand to his cheek.

Mihara crossed his arms and looked vaguely out at the sea, as if an explanation might be found there. The pale outline of the peninsula was visible across the bay.

'Inspector Mihara,' said Torigai abruptly. He had decided it was the right time to bring up something that had been weighing on his mind. 'Why exactly have the Tokyo Police suddenly taken such an interest in Sayama's suicide?'

Mihara did not reply immediately. First, he produced a cigarette and offered it to Torigai. He lit it, and then his own, before slowly exhaling a pale cloud of smoke.

'Inspector Torigai, you've been very helpful, so I'll let you in on this,' he began. 'Kenichi Sayama was a key witness in the bribery investigation at Ministry X. He might only have been an assistant section chief, but he had years of practical experience under his belt and knew a great deal about how the place was run. Which is to say, he was seriously implicated in this scandal. In fact, he was probably more of a suspect than a witness. But the details of the case were only just coming to light, and we failed to keep a close enough eye on our man. And then he went and died on us.'

Mihara tapped the ash from his cigarette and went on:

'With him gone, all sorts of people will be breathing a sigh of relief. In fact, the more we investigate, the more we're realizing just how much he must have known. I can't tell you what a blow it was, losing a precious witness like that. But while we're moping about it, others are jumping for joy. Now, maybe Sayama really did kill himself just to protect them, but we've begun to have suspicions about his suicide.'

'Suspicions?'

'Basically, we're wondering if he committed suicide willingly. Somebody could have forced him into it.'

Torigai looked intently at him. 'Do you have any evidence?'

'Nothing concrete,' replied Mihara. 'But he didn't leave a suicide note – and, if I'm not mistaken, neither did the woman.'

This was true. Torigai had mentioned as much to the chief.

'Also, we looked into Sayama's private life in Tokyo, but we couldn't find anything linking him to Toki.'

'What? Nothing?'

'Well, we did learn that he had a mistress, but we haven't been able to establish whether it was her. As for Toki herself, I visited the Koyuki to ask the waitresses about her, and the apartment block where she lived, and it seems she did have a lover. There was a man who often called the concierge, asking for her, and she would often spend the night away. The thing is, he never actually visited her apartment, so we've been unable to work out who he was. It may well have been Sayama, but there's no solid evidence.'

Torigai found this a little odd. Hadn't Sayama and Toki committed suicide together? 'But think about it, Inspector,' he said to Mihara. 'Two waitresses from the Koyuki saw Sayama and Toki boarding the Asakaze together. There was even a third witness, a customer from the restaurant. Three witnesses. And then they committed suicide together, right here. I attended the scene myself, and there are the photos you brought from the station, not to mention the autopsy report.'

'Exactly,' replied Mihara, looking perplexed for the first time. 'Now that I'm here, looking at all the evidence, I realize it must have been a double suicide after all. That's what's bothering me. I arrived from Tokyo armed with all these suspicions, but none of them tally with the facts.'

Torigai felt like he was beginning to understand what kind of suspicions Mihara was referring to.

4

'Shall we make our way back?' said Mihara. The two of them got up and, walking side by side, headed back the way they had come.

At the Nishitetsu station, a thought occurred to Torigai. 'You know, there's another Kashii station, on the main line. It's five hundred metres from here. In fact, I dug up some information around here that might interest you.'

He told Mihara about the two couples that had been spotted, one at each station, on the night of the twentieth. Then he explained how he had timed himself walking between the two stations.

'Intriguing,' said Mihara, his eyes lighting up. 'Why don't you show me what you mean?' And so, just as Torigai had done previously, the two men walked between the mainline station and the Nishitetsu station at three different speeds.

'I see. Even walking fairly slowly, it would have taken them no more than seven minutes,' said Mihara, looking at his watch. 'Eleven is too long. Unless, of course, they stopped somewhere.'

'Or they might have been two separate couples.'

'True, true. But . . .' Mihara began, looking pensively up at the sky. 'Something tells me they were the same two people. They got off at the mainline station, walked past the Nishitetsu station and headed to that spot on the beach . . .'

Torigai told him the details of the statements he'd taken from the passengers, and from the station employee who'd been on duty on the evening in question. Mihara noted everything down carefully.

'Hard to say either way, isn't it? But I have to say, Inspector Torigai, this is getting interesting. Got our work cut out for us, haven't we?' he said, sympathetically eyeing the thin, elderly Torigai.

The following evening, Torigai was seeing Mihara off on the platform at Hakata station. The inspector was travelling back to Tokyo on the Unzen, an express that departed at 6.02.

'When will you get to Tokyo?'

'Tomorrow afternoon, at 3.40.'

'Ah. You'll be exhausted.'

'Thank you for everything. You've been a great help.' Mihara bowed slightly, his youthful face breaking into a smile.

'Oh no, I can't imagine I was much use to you,' replied Torigai.

'On the contrary, Inspector Torigai. You made my trip to Kyushu worthwhile.' Mihara seemed very sincere and looked Torigai in the eye as he spoke.

It was still twelve minutes until the Unzen, arriving from Naga-saki, was due at the station. The two men waited side by side. Trains were constantly arriving and departing in front of them. A freight train was waiting at the platform opposite. All around them was the hustle and bustle of a large train station. Mihara's expression hinted at the vague melancholy that long journeys, like the one he faced back to Tokyo, have a habit of producing.

'I imagine the platforms at Tokyo station are similarly packed,' said Torigai. He had never seen the capital's central station but pictured it to himself now.

'Absolutely. It's quite the scene, you know – trains endlessly coming and going.' Mihara made this remark casually, but as soon as the words were out of his mouth he startled as if he'd received an electric shock. He had just hit upon a crucial fact.

At Tokyo station, those witnesses had seen Toki and Sayama getting on the train together. As he recalled, they had been standing on platform 13, from which they had spotted the Asakaze at platform 15. But at Tokyo station, there were two train lines – tracks 13 and 14 – in between these two platforms. At a station like that, where trains arrived and departed so frequently, what were the chances a person could actually stand on platform 13 and still see a train at platform 15, without another train pulling up and blocking the view?

6. The Four-Minute Interval

Kiichi Mihara arrived in Tokyo late in the afternoon. His long journey from Kyushu had left him craving a decent cup of coffee. He passed through the ticket gate and took a taxi straight to Ginza, where he hurried to his favourite café.

'Mihara-san! Been a while, hasn't it?' said one of the waitresses in greeting.

He normally came here for a coffee every couple of days, so it was only natural for her to say this after his almost week-long absence. Of course, she knew nothing of his trip to Kyushu.

He recognized a few regulars. The place hadn't changed in the slightest while he was away. For the waitress and customers alike, life at the café had been carrying on as usual. On the other side of the window, the streets of Ginza seemed unchanged, too. It was as though, for the five or six days he'd been away, he alone had been thrust from this world. Nobody here knew what Mihara had been up to during the intervening days – and, despite the unusual things he had seen, nobody showed even a passing interest in him. Of course, this was only natural, and yet it left him feeling strangely lonely.

The coffee was delicious. It was the one thing he missed whenever he left the capital. Next, Mihara took his bag, got up and hailed a taxi back towards Tokyo Police headquarters.

He opened a door whose nameplate read 'Inspector Kasai, Second Investigative Division', and walked into the office to find his boss sitting at the desk.

'I'm back, sir.'

Inspector Kasai turned to greet Mihara, his bull neck bulging slightly as he smiled. 'Good to see you. Must have been a long trip!'

Everyone else was out, except for a young detective, who brought Mihara some tea.

'How did it go?'

'Here,' Mihara opened his bag and took out the materials relating to Sayama and Toki's suicide that he'd borrowed from the Fukuoka Police. 'Take a look. A classic love suicide, that's their verdict.'

'Hmm . . .' Kasai carefully perused the various photos, the autopsy results and the crime-scene report. 'So it *was* a double suicide after all,' he murmured, setting the documents back down. He spoke with an air of resignation, as if it were time to give up the chase.

'Sorry to send you all that way for nothing,' he added, looking back up at Mihara.

'Actually, it wasn't a complete waste of time.'

Kasai looked slightly taken aback. 'What do you mean?'

'I learned a few interesting things.'

'Oh?'

'This isn't the official line from the Fukuoka Police, but one of their old hands, an inspector by the name of Torigai, had some intriguing details to share.' Mihara explained the theory of the dining-car receipt, as well as the experiment they had conducted by walking between the two Kashii stations.

'Hmm. The receipt idea is certainly interesting,' said Kasai, after some thought. 'So Toki could have left the train at Atami or Shizuoka, then spent four or five days in that area before heading to Fukuoka and telephoning Sayama, who was already at the inn. That's the theory, is it?'

'Yes.'

'In that case, we need to work out why Sayama dropped Toki off along the way, and what he had her do in the four or five days she was in Atami or Shizuoka.'

'Chief, does this mean we're on the same page here?' The two men looked each other straight in the eye. 'I mean, the evidence makes it clear this was a double suicide. But do you agree that there could be something else going on?'

Kasai's expression became distant for a moment. 'Mihara, we could be wrong about this. Sayama's death was such a huge blow to the bribery investigation that now we've decided even his suicide is worthy of suspicion. We mustn't descend into amateurish sleuthing.'

It was true; an investigation fuelled by instinct alone could be a slippery slope. But Mihara knew he needed to discover the truth behind the double suicide. If he searched and searched and still found nothing, he'd be happy to call it a day. But if he stopped now, the case would never leave him in peace.

When Mihara explained this, the chief nodded his agreement.

'Well then, let's give it our best shot, even if it turns out we're aiming at the wrong target,' he said, folding his arms. 'Listen. The Asakaze is a super-express, isn't it? That means even third-class seats require a reservation. If Toki got off somewhere along the way, she'll have left an empty seat. We should look into that. I'll have someone question the guard from the train.'

2

The next day, Kiichi Mihara went to Tokyo station. He felt clear-headed and in good spirits, probably because he'd slept so well. He was still at the age when tiredness could be cured by a single good night's sleep.

He climbed the steps to platform 13, where he stood for over an hour, gazing at the Yaesu exit on the other side of the platforms, almost as if he was waiting for someone.

Except it wasn't quite true to say he was gazing at the exit, because his view was continuously obscured by passing trains. At platform 13, long electric-powered commuter trains were constantly coming and going on the Yokusuka line, while regular locomotives frequently departed from platform 14. The result was that, from where he was standing on platform 13, he never had a clear view of platform 15. Even when a commuter train departed from the platform in front of him, there would always be another train standing on the other side. This being the first station on that line, that train would often wait a long time to depart, and when it did finally move off, another would just be pulling in on the Yokosuka line. In other words, the tracks between platforms 13 and 15 were constantly occupied, and there was simply no way of seeing all the way across to the latter.

Mihara had come here because of what Jūtarō Torigai had said while they were waiting for Mihara's train at Hakata station. Acting on a hunch, he had decided to conduct this experiment.

It was strange. He'd been standing here for over an hour, staring, and was yet to catch even a glimpse of platform 15. What could it mean? The witnesses had definitely been standing on platform 13, and the Asakaze had departed from platform 15. Could the tracks really have been clear, even for the brief interval in which they supposedly saw Sayama and Toki boarding the train?

Mihara pondered this for a moment, then walked slowly along the platform and down the steps towards the station offices.

He found the stationmaster, introduced himself, and asked:

'This might seem an odd question, but if you were on platform 13, would it be possible to see the 6.30 Asakaze while it's standing at platform 15?' The stationmaster had greying hair. He looked at Mihara with a bemused expression.

'See the Asakaze . . .? Oh, you mean, is there a time when the tracks are clear?'

'Exactly.'

'Hmm. I'd think there would usually be a train blocking the view, but let me check for you. Just a moment, please,' he said, unfolding a station chart on his desk. With a finger he traced several of the intricate, seemingly countless lines that criss-crossed the paper. 'Here we are! It looks like there *is* an interval – a pretty short interval, mind you – when there are no trains on tracks 13 and 14 and you'd be able to see the Asakaze at platform 15. Who'd have thought it!' the stationmaster exclaimed, as if he had discovered something remarkable.

'I see. So there is a gap?' asked Mihara, a little disappointed. But what the stationmaster said next rekindled his attention.

'Yes – but it only lasts four minutes.'

'Four minutes?' Mihara's pulse quickened. 'How does that work?'

'Let me explain,' began the stationmaster. 'The Asakaze arrives at platform 15 at 5.49 and departs at 6.30, so it's at the platform for a total of forty-one minutes. Now let's look at what happens on tracks 13 and 14 in the meantime. On track 13, a Yokosuka line train arrives at 5.46 and leaves at 5.57. Shortly afterwards, at 6.01, another one pulls in, then sets off at 6.12. But even after that, there's a Shizuoka-bound train at platform 14 which arrives at 6.05 and stays there until 6.35, blocking the view of the Asakaze.'

Unable to take all this in at once, Mihara got out his notebook. The stationmaster noticed and said, 'Bit hard to follow, isn't it? Let me write you a summary.' He noted the various train times down on a piece of paper, then handed it to Mihara.

3

Back at the police station, Mihara looked at the timetable the stationmaster had written out for him, then took an envelope from his desk drawer and drew the following on the back of it.

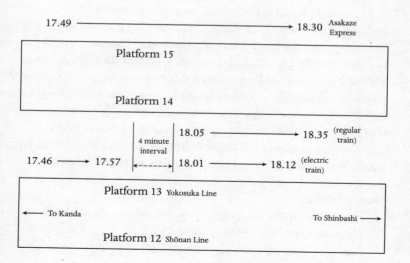

57

This made things a lot clearer. The train at platform 13 left at 5.57, after which there was a gap of four minutes when the Asakaze would be visible before the next train arrived at 6.01. In other words, the witnesses who had seen Sayama and Toki boarding the Asakaze must have been on platform 13 during those four minutes.

It was at this point that Mihara realized the true importance of the testimony given by those witnesses. Their claim that Sayama and Toki had boarded the Asakaze together while chatting away merrily was practically the only piece of evidence holding the love suicide theory together. There was nothing else, on the surface at least, to demonstrate conclusively that the two had been intimate. Though both Sayama and Toki had been known to have a lover, the only people who had actually seen them together were these witnesses, who, by chance, had been standing on platform 13 during that four-minute interval.

What an extraordinary coincidence that they were standing there at precisely that moment, thought Mihara. But soon another thought flashed through his mind: had it really only been a coincidence?

Speculating on these sorts of chance occurrences was a risky business. But a window of only four minutes? Somehow, Mihara felt there had to be more to this.

He thought about the witnesses: two waitresses from the Koyuki and one of their regular customers. The customer was on his way to Kamakura, and the waitresses had been seeing him off on platform 13. Then they had spotted Sayama and Toki boarding the Asakaze. Mihara had learned all this when he'd questioned Yaeko, one of the waitresses in question, before leaving for Fukuoka. At the time, he hadn't ascribed much importance to her account, but now he realized he needed to visit her again and run over a few things.

When Mihara arrived at the Koyuki later that morning, he found Yaeko busy cleaning, clad in a pair of baggy work trousers.

'Oh dear – I can't believe you're seeing me like this!' she said, blushing slightly.

'Thank you again for helping me the other day,' said Mihara. 'You'll remember you were telling me how you and another waitress were seeing a customer off at Tokyo station when you spotted Sayama and Toki.'

'That's right,' she said, nodding.

'I completely forgot to ask. What was the customer's name?'

Yaeko gave him a sharp look. Mihara understood her hesitation. She was reluctant to get one of the restaurant's precious regulars into trouble.

'Don't worry. I won't cause him any bother. I'm just making sure I have the details right,' he said.

'His name is Tatsuo Yasuda,' she said, dropping her voice.

'Tatsuo Yasuda. And his occupation?'

'He said he owned a big machinery company over in Nihonbashi.'

'I see. Has he been coming here for a while, then?'

'Three or four years. Toki was usually the one who waited on him.'

'So that's why he knew her. Tell me, when you were on the platform, who was it who saw her first?'

'Mr Yasuda. He said, "Isn't that Toki?" and pointed her out to us.'

'Ah, did he? I see.' Mihara fell silent. He seemed to be considering his next question – or perhaps there was something else weighing on his mind.

4

After a pause, Mihara smiled and asked, 'When you and Tomiko saw Mr Yasuda off at the station that day, was that a spur-of-the-moment decision?

'Yes. We were out eating at the time. The Coq d'Or, in Ginza,' replied Yaeko.

'Ah, took you out for a meal, did he? I assume that part, at least, had been planned in advance?'

'Yes, Mr Yasuda was here at the restaurant the night before, and he invited us to meet him in Ginza at half past three the following afternoon.'

'Half past three, I see. And then?'

'Well, as we were finishing our meal, Mr Yasuda told us he was heading to Kamakura and wanted us to see him off at the station. So Tomiko and I did as he asked.'

'And what sort of time was that?'

'Hmm, let me think . . .' Yaeko cocked her head and squinted as she tried to remember. 'Ah, yes. I asked him what train he was getting, and he said the 6.12 on the Yokosuka line. He pointed out that it was 5.35 and we'd make it in time as long as we went straight to the station.'

'The 6.12 on the Yokosuka line,' said Mihara, recalling the diagram he had sketched the previous evening. The 6.12 arrived at platform 13 at 6.01. Yasuda had been able to see the Asakaze at platform 15, so they must have arrived before 6.01. Now we're getting to the important part, thought Mihara.

'When you got to platform 13, Mr Yasuda's train hadn't yet pulled in, correct?'

'That's right,' Yaeko answered immediately.

'So you must have got there around six o'clock, or slightly earlier,' Mihara murmured, more to himself than to Yaeko.

'Yes. The clock on the platform showed a few minutes to six.'

'I see. Very observant of you to notice that.'

'Well, in the taxi, Mr Yasuda kept glancing at his wristwatch. In the end, even we were anxious for him to catch the 6.12!'

This detail caught Mihara's attention. 'He kept glancing at his watch, you say?'

'Yes, he wouldn't stop! Even when we were still at the Coq d'Or.'

At this, Mihara sank into thought. Even after he'd left Yaeko and boarded a bus, his mind continued to whirl. Yasuda had been checking his watch. Had he simply been worrying about missing his train? Or was there something else he didn't want to miss – for example, that four-minute interval?

If he wanted a clear view of the Asakaze, he had to be there no earlier and no later than that four-minute window. Too early, and the 5.57 Yokosuka line train would have been waiting at the platform, leaving him no choice but to take it to Kamakura. Too late, and the 6.01 would have arrived, blocking the view of the Asakaze. Could

Yasuda have been checking his watch so frequently because he was aiming for those four minutes?

I might be jumping to conclusions here, thought Mihara, trying to rein in his suspicion. But the more he tried to dismiss this idea, the stronger its hold on him grew.

Why would Yasuda have gone to all this trouble? If Mihara followed his theory to its logical conclusion, the answer was simple. Yasuda wanted to ensure that the waitresses saw Sayama and Toki boarding the train. In other words, he was discreetly creating two witnesses.

Mihara's heart was beating faster now. The figure of Tatsuo Yasuda seemed to loom in his mind. I need to meet him, he thought.

And indeed, later that same day, Mihara paid a visit to Yasuda's office. The afternoon sun streamed in through the window of the reception room where he was waiting. Tatsuo Yasuda walked into the room and, Mihara's business card in his hand and a serene smile on his face, gestured for him to sit down.

7. Chance or Design?

I

'Very sorry to bother you. I just have a few questions to ask – on rather a strange subject,' began Mihara.

'Of course. Please, ask away.' Yasuda offered him one of the cigarettes that were left out on the table for guests, before taking one for himself and lighting both with his lighter. Yasuda had a calm, easy manner. He must have been around forty, with round, rosy cheeks, slightly curly hair and large, friendly eyes. He seemed to glow with all the confidence of a successful businessman.

'Well, it's in relation to the double suicide involving Kenichi Sayama, the assistant section chief at Ministry X. I'm sure you've seen it in the papers.'

Yasuda nodded emphatically as he puffed on his cigarette. 'Oh, I didn't just see it in the papers. I knew Mr Sayama personally – we did business together. My company supplies machinery to Ministry X, you see.'

Mihara hadn't realized that Yasuda's company was connected to the ministry.

'Such a shame, isn't it? Mr Sayama was a good man, a real professional. I never would have thought him the type to get involved in a love suicide,' said Yasuda. His words seemed laden with genuine feeling.

'Yes. About Mr Sayama . . .' began Mihara. He reached into his pocket and then, after some hesitation, decided not to pull out his notebook. 'A waitress at the Koyuki restaurant told me you saw him boarding a train with a woman at Tokyo station.'

62

'Indeed I did,' said Yasuda, leaning forward. 'It was early evening, and I was on my way to Kamakura. The waitresses from the Koyuki came to see me off. That was when I saw Mr Sayama and Toki on the platform opposite, about to board the express. I pointed them out to the waitresses. I knew both of them separately, so it came as quite a surprise. I never would have suspected they were intimate like that. I remember thinking to myself: it really is a small world.' Yasuda was squinting slightly, perhaps because of the cigarette smoke. 'Little did I know they were off to meet their deaths. All very sad, really. Just goes to show that romance is best enjoyed in moderation, don't you think?' Yasuda flashed a charming smile.

'Mr Sayama never visited the Koyuki, then?' asked Mihara.

'No, I don't think so. I often take clients there, but never Mr Sayama. People start to talk if you go around inviting government officials to dinner.' He laughed. 'And I'm not just saying that because you're with the police. The ministry is in hot water these days, what with the bribery scandal and everything.'

'It's been suggested that Mr Sayama committed suicide to take the heat off his superiors. Do you think Toki could have gone along with the suicide out of sympathy?'

'I wouldn't know about that,' replied Yasuda. His expression seemed to imply that such speculation was Mihara's job, not his. 'But it did surprise me that the two of them were involved with each other. I had no idea!'

'Did you know Toki well, then?'

'Well, she usually served my room at the restaurant, so yes, you could say I knew her quite well. Not in the way you might be thinking, though. Our relationship ended at the door of the Koyuki. So I suppose you could say I knew her without really knowing her. After all, I didn't even realize she was Sayama's mistress.'

Mihara had one more question, an important one. 'Do you often go to Kamakura?'

Yasuda smiled, briefly showing his teeth. 'Well, yes. My wife lives there.'

'Your wife?'

'She has tuberculosis, you see. We've been living separately for a while now. I've rented her a house in Gokuraku-ji, with an elderly maid to look after her. I drop by to see her about once a week.'

'You must worry about her.'

Yasuda bowed slightly to thank him for his concern. Mihara felt there was something else he should ask but couldn't put his finger on what it might be.

'Well, I'm sorry to have bothered you like this,' he said, getting to his feet.

Yasuda also rose from his seat. 'Not at all. I'm not sure how helpful I've been, but if there's anything else I can do, please don't hesitate,' he said, his round eyes narrowing as he smiled again.

Outside, the weather was fine. As he walked along the street, Mihara thought: Yasuda knew about that four-minute interval. He must have discovered it during his frequent trips to see his wife in Kamakura. Or at least, that has to be a possibility . . .

2

Back at the office, Mihara went to see Inspector Kasai. He was there not to make a formal report but simply to explain his theory of the four-minute interval, believing it might be of interest. He also mentioned his meeting with Yasuda.

Kasai was even more intrigued than he'd expected. 'Sounds like quite the discovery,' he said, clasping his hands together on the desk. 'That completely passed us by, didn't it?'

Seeing Kasai's excitement, Mihara took from his pocket the diagram he'd made of the movements of trains at platforms 13, 14 and 15 between 5.57 and 6.01. He handed it to Kasai, who inspected it carefully.

'I see. Yes, that all makes sense. You know, this is very good work,' he said, looking up at Mihara.

It's not me you should be praising, thought Mihara, it's Inspector Torigai of the Fukuoka Police. Without that hint from the veteran detective, he would never have discovered any of this.

'The question now is whether these four-minute witnesses were there on that platform by chance or design.'

Four-minute witnesses. *Chance or design*. Mihara had to admire the chief's way with words. Kasai asked him to run through the details again, then wrote down the following.

1. Yasuda invited the two waitresses from the Koyuki out to an early meal, and thereby got them to accompany him to Tokyo station.
2. Yasuda kept looking at his watch, even when they were eating at the restaurant.
3. They arrived at platform 13 just in time for the four-minute interval.
4. It was Yasuda who spotted Sayama and Toki, before pointing them out to the waitresses.

Once Kasai had finished writing, he studied the piece of paper carefully, tapping his pencil against his cheek like a schoolboy.

'Yes,' he said, after a moment. 'There's no way this happened by chance. Yasuda must have planned the whole thing.' Kasai had an excited glint in his eyes.

'Sir, this changes things, doesn't it?'

'It does.' Kasai's reply seemed almost automatic, but then he closed his eyes as if to think. After a moment, he called out to a nearby detective: 'Listen – Ministry X buys machinery from a company owned by Tatsuo Yasuda. Find out how deep their relationship goes, would you?'

'Understood,' said the detective, taking the name down in a notebook as he left.

'Now, let's see . . .' Kasai looked back over his notes carefully, then lit a cigarette. 'If Yasuda did plan the whole thing, the next question is why.'

People only laid plans they expected to benefit from. What did Yasuda stand to gain by creating witnesses to Sayama and Toki's departure?

'He needed a third party to witness the scene,' suggested Mihara, after some thought.

'A third party?'

'Yes. It wouldn't do for Yasuda alone to see them. There had to be someone else.'

'Are you saying Yasuda wasn't a third party to all this?'

'That would be the implication,' replied Mihara, with a look that said that in fact it was all but certain. Kasai seemed lost in thought.

'Let's run through this again,' said the chief eventually. 'Sayama and Toki committed suicide near Hakata. They left Tokyo on an express train. Yasuda arranged for two women to see them boarding the train together, creating these third-party witnesses you mentioned. Hmm, this doesn't make sense . . .'

Mihara knew what Kasai was getting at. If the pair in question were planning to commit suicide together anyway, it seemed pointless to create witnesses to their departure. Did this mean, then, that Yasuda had something to do with the suicide? If so, what? Mihara was asking himself the same questions.

'In any case, there's more to this than meets the eye.'

'Indeed,' replied Kasai, nodding. 'When you gather the facts, they all point to Yasuda having planned this. But the motive is missing. Every plan needs a motive but, right now, it's not clear what Yasuda was trying to achieve.'

'We just need to work out why he thought this plan necessary in the first place,' said Mihara.

'You're right,' replied Kasai. The two men looked at each other excitedly. 'Any idea why Yasuda would deliberately aim for that four-minute interval when the Asakaze is visible from platform 13? If all he wanted was to show them the train, couldn't he just have taken them straight to platform 15?' he asked, as if testing Mihara.

'That part I've figured out. Platform 15 is only for long-distance trains, so taking them there would have seemed too deliberate. Far more natural for him to say he was going to Kamakura and show them the train from platform 13. The reason he took such care over the four-minute interval was precisely because he wanted everything to seem entirely unplanned.'

Kasai smiled, which meant he agreed. 'Ah, by the way, we've heard from the guard who was on the Asakaze on the fourteenth of January.'

'Oh?' said Mihara, leaning forward.

'Unfortunately, he doesn't remember any empty seats. Says it's too long ago to recall. Fat lot of use, wasn't he! If only he'd remembered, we'd know where Toki got off that train.'

8. Hokkaido and Kyushu

I

When Mihara came into work the next morning, he found the chief already at his desk.

'Morning, sir.'

Kasai looked up from his documents. 'Ah, morning. Listen,' he said, beckoning Mihara over. 'Have you recovered from that Kyushu trip yet?' he asked. He was drinking tea from a large cup, the kind usually seen in sushi restaurants.

'Yes. A couple of nights' sleep was all I needed,' replied Mihara with a smile.

'I'd have preferred to give you some leave, but we're a little busy for that. I'm afraid you'll just have to stick it out.'

'Not a problem.'

'Anyway, about Yasuda,' said Kasai, cutting to the chase. 'Take a seat.' Mihara sat down on the other side of Kasai's desk.

'I had some digging done. It would seem he and the ministry are pretty cosy with each other.'

'Ah. Just as we suspected.'

'It's not like he's selling them vast quantities of machinery, but I'm told he's on particularly good terms with Yoshio Ishida there.'

'Ishida?' Mihara glanced at his superior. Yoshio Ishida was a major figure at Ministry X – and the head of the division currently being investigated for bribery. Within the ministry, he had a reputation as an intelligent man who knew how to get the job done, but the police had marked him as a key suspect.

'Yes, Ishida. The two of them are very close, I'm told. Could be significant, don't you think?'

'Definitely.'

Yasuda's face was still fresh in Mihara's mind from their meeting the day before. He had come across as a sharp-witted man. Those eyes, large and friendly and always on the move, were those of a shrewd industrialist. It was easy to imagine his self-assured manner exerting a sort of intense pressure on those around him. Yesterday, Mihara had even found him quite intimidating. It seemed entirely plausible that a man like that could get himself into the good books of someone like Ishida if he set his mind to it.

'What about the relationship between Yasuda and Sayama?' asked Mihara.

'I'd been wondering about that too. But it turns out the two of them weren't particularly close,' said Kasai, holding his cup of tea in both hands. 'As assistant chief, Sayama was heavily involved in the section's day-to-day affairs, so he and Yasuda certainly crossed paths. But it doesn't look like they ever stepped outside the bounds of a regular business relationship. There's no sign of any underhand dealings between them.'

'Hmm, I see.' Mihara took the cigarette Kasai had offered him and lit it.

'What do you reckon, then? Should we take a closer look at Yasuda?' Kasai thrust his head forward, a gesture which usually signalled his enthusiasm.

'I think we should. I'd like to take a crack at this,' replied Mihara, noting Kasai's eagerness.

'Chance or design: that's what it all comes down to, isn't it?' said Kasai, referring to their conversation the day before. He was in a good mood now.

'It has to be by design, surely. Those four minutes . . . I just don't see how that could be a coincidence.'

'Yesterday you said that if we could just work out why Yasuda thought all this was necessary, that would lead us to his motive.'

'That's right.'

'So, why did Yasuda need someone other than himself to witness

Sayama and Toki setting off on this fateful journey of theirs? Your theory was that he wanted to create witnesses without it seeming intentional, wasn't it?'

'Exactly. I don't see any other explanation.'

'I'm with you on that,' said Kasai. 'Well, I want you to tackle this however you see fit.'

Mihara stubbed his cigarette out in the ashtray. 'Understood. I'll give it my best shot,' he said, bowing slightly.

But the chief seemed reluctant to let him go. 'Where are you going to start?' he asked. His tone was nonchalant, but his expression betrayed his curiosity.

'I want to find out exactly what Yasuda did, and where he went, between the nineteenth and the twenty-first of January,' said Mihara.

'The nineteenth to the twenty-first . . .' Kasai looked away pensively for a moment. 'Ah. The bodies were found in Kashii on the morning of the twenty-first, so you want to establish Yasuda's movements over the previous two days. Two days is about how long it takes to get from Tokyo to Kyushu, isn't it?'

'Exactly. Come to think of it, maybe I should look into the twenty-second too, to account for the journey back to Tokyo.'

'How long is it from Tokyo to Hakata on an express?'

'Usually just over twenty hours. On a super-express like the Asakaze it's more like seventeen.'

'I see. So forty hours or so for the round trip.' His cigarette still between his fingers, Kasai rubbed his eye with his thumb, as though deep in thought.

2

Mihara was shown to the same reception room as the day before. A young woman brought him some tea and asked him to wait while Yasuda finished the call he was on. The man seemed in no hurry to arrive. Mihara found himself staring at a still-life painting hanging on the wall, wondering just how long a business call could take. When Yasuda walked in, he was beaming.

'So sorry to keep you waiting.'

Just like the day before, Mihara felt slightly intimidated by Yasuda's presence. 'My apologies for bothering you again,' he said, getting to his feet.

'Not at all. Sorry for the delay – my call went on a little longer than I expected,' replied Yasuda with complete composure, a friendly look in his eyes.

'Glad to hear business is keeping you so busy.'

'Thank you, but it wasn't a business call. I was phoning my home in Kamakura.'

'Ah, your wife, I presume?' Mihara remembered Yasuda telling him yesterday that his wife was convalescing there.

'Her maid, actually. My wife's condition has got worse lately. I can't visit Kamakura every day, so I phone to see how she's getting on,' replied Yasuda, a smile still on his face.

'You must be rather worried.'

'Thank you for your concern.'

'Well, Mr Yasuda, I just have a few more questions for you,' said Mihara, trying to change the subject as casually as possible.

'Of course. What is it you'd like to ask?' asked Yasuda. There was no trace of unease on his face.

'This is some time ago, but were you in Tokyo between the twentieth and the twenty-second of January this year? I'm just trying to get a few details straight.'

Yasuda laughed. 'Oh dear, taking me for a suspect now, are you?'

'Not at all. Just filling in some gaps.'

Mihara had thought Yasuda might comment on the fact that these dates coincided with Sayama's suicide, but he did nothing of the sort. It was not clear from his expression what, if anything, the three-day period meant to him.

'The twentieth of January?' he said, closing his eyes to think. Then he took a small notebook from the desk drawer and flicked through its pages. 'Ah, here we are. I was in Hokkaido.'

'Hokkaido?'

'Sapporo, to be precise. We have a major client up there, the Futaba company. I was visiting them. I stayed in Hokkaido four days and was back in Tokyo on the twenty-fifth,' said Yasuda, still consulting his notebook.

Hokkaido . . . Mihara's expression had gone blank. That was the opposite end of the country to Kyushu!

'Would more detail be helpful?' asked Yasuda, his eyes crinkling with a smile as he looked up at Mihara.

'Yes, if you don't mind,' replied Mihara, taking out his notebook and a pencil.

'I left Tokyo on the Towada Express, which departs from Ueno station at 7.15 p.m.'

'Can I ask if you were travelling alone?'

'Yes. I usually do when I'm on business.'

'I see. Please go on.'

'I arrived at Aomori the next morning at 9.09. Then I transferred to the Seikan ferry to Hakodate, which leaves at 9.50,' began Yasuda, reading the details from his notebook. 'The ferry arrives in Hakodate at 2.20. There's a connection there with the Nemuro-bound express train – that's the Marimo, which leaves at 2.50. I arrived in Sapporo at 8.34 that evening. A man named Kawanishi from the Futaba company came to meet me, then showed me to the inn where I was staying, the Marusō. That was the evening of the twenty-first. I stayed there until the twenty-fourth, when I left Hokkaido, and I was back in Tokyo on the twenty-fifth.'

Mihara wrote all this down in his notebook. When he had finished, Yasuda, smile still firmly in place, asked: 'Well, is that helpful?'

'Yes, that's all very clear, thank you,' replied Mihara, flashing a smile of his own.

'I see your work is keeping you rather busy, too. No stone left unturned, eh?' Yasuda spoke calmly, but Mihara thought he detected a hint of sarcasm in his voice.

'Please don't take this the wrong way. It's just a routine enquiry.'

'Of course! I understand entirely. If there's anything else you need to know, just ask.'

'Sorry for bothering you like this.'

Yasuda saw him to the exit. He seemed entirely unruffled by the encounter.

Before heading back to police headquarters, Mihara dropped into his usual café in Ginza. After ordering a coffee, he took out his notebook and wrote out a summary of everything Yasuda had told him.

20 Jan.:   Dep. Ueno 7.15 p.m. (Towada)
21 Jan.:   Arr. Aomori 9.09 a.m.
             Dep. Aomori 9.50 a.m. (Seikan ferry). Arr. Hakodate
             2.20 p.m.
             Dep. Hakodate 2.50 p.m. (Marimo). Arr. Sapporo
             8.34 p.m. (met at station)
21–4 Jan.:   Stays at Marusō inn. Dep. 24 Jan.
25 Jan.:   Arr. Tokyo

As Mihara was studying what he had written, the waitress serving his coffee looked over his shoulder and asked:

'Planning a trip to Hokkaido, are you, Mihara-san?'

'Something like that . . .' replied Mihara, with a vague smile.

'Well, isn't that nice! You were in Kyushu just the other day, and now Hokkaido? Imagine zipping up and down the country like that!'

It was true, thought Mihara. The case now stretched from one end of Japan to the other.

3

Back at headquarters, Mihara went to Kasai's office to report. After relaying Yasuda's story, he showed the chief the itinerary he'd written out.

'Hmm . . .' said Kasai, eagerly examining Mihara's notes. 'Hokkaido, of all places! But that's the other end of the country to Kyushu . . .'

'I know. Bit disappointing, isn't it?' said Mihara. He really did feel quite let down by this discovery.

'But is it true, I wonder?' said Kasai, his chin resting in his hand.

'Yasuda is a smart man. He wouldn't lie about something this easy to verify. I think we can assume he's telling the truth.'

'Right. But we still need proof.'

'Of course. I could ask the Sapporo Police to check his story with the man from the Futaba company who came to meet him at the station, and with the Marusō inn.'

'Good. Yes, do that.'

As Mihara got up to leave, the chief stopped him. 'One more thing. What's Yasuda's family situation?'

'He's married. But his wife has tuberculosis and lives in a separate residence, in Kamakura.'

'Ah yes, you mentioned that yesterday. You were saying his frequent trips to Kamakura might have led him to discover that four-minute interval at the station.'

'Yes. When I visited him today, he'd just been on the phone to her. Apparently, her condition has worsened.'

'So he lives alone in Tokyo, then?'

Mihara had looked into this. 'Yes, he has his own house in the Asagaya district, with two maids to look after him.' Kasai looked thoughtful but said nothing.

Next, Mihara sent a long telegram to the Sapporo Police. The reply would probably come tomorrow, or the day after. Not that he was expecting much from it. Yasuda seemed far too shrewd to lie blatantly about his movements.

Now that all he could do now was wait for a reply to his telegram, Mihara was at a loose end. He began to feel oddly frustrated.

Perhaps as a result of this restlessness, a new doubt began to form in his mind. Was Yasuda's wife really convalescing in Kamakura?

He didn't suspect her of any connection to the case. At the same time, Mihara simply couldn't shake that four-minute window from his mind. He'd assumed Yasuda had learned of its existence through his repeated trips to see his wife, who – he claimed – was living in Kamakura. But now Mihara was beginning to doubt this part of Yasuda's story. What if it was not his wife he had been visiting in Kamakura, but someone else? The Hokkaido trip would probably check out, for the simple reason that Yasuda was expecting them to investigate it. But the convalescing wife? It was such a banal story they'd swallowed it without a moment's thought. Now that Mihara thought about it, they'd left a gaping hole in their investigation.

We need to tread carefully here, thought Mihara.

He went to see Kasai again, but his chief was out somewhere. Mihara left a note on the desk saying he was going to Kamakura, then made his way out of the building. If he left Tokyo now, he could be back by late evening.

He bought a box of cakes from a well-known shop at Tokyo station. If Yasuda's wife really was ill, he would need a gift.

Mihara headed to platform 13 and boarded the train that happened to be standing there. Even now, he noted, his view of platform 15 was blocked by his train and the one at platform 14.

That four-minute interval was quite the clever trick, thought Mihara to himself once again. It could never have happened by chance. No, Yasuda must have planned it.

And now Mihara realized why. *Yasuda knew he would be investigated at some point.* That had to be it. He had ensured the waitresses from the Koyuki were there because he needed someone other than himself to witness the scene.

The train moved off. During the hour or so it took to reach Kamakura, thoughts continued to swirl around Mihara's mind. Yasuda had certainly acted suspiciously, but what was he actually trying to achieve? Why go to such trouble to create witnesses? Was this really anything other than a double suicide? Yasuda's motive simply wasn't clear.

And then there was the fact that, on the evening of the twentieth, when Sayama and Toki had committed suicide, Yasuda had been on his way to Hokkaido, arriving the following day. Kyushu and Hokkaido. How could those two distant places possibly be connected?

At Kamakura station, Mihara changed to a local Enoshima line train. His carriage was filled by a group of schoolchildren on a trip, chirruping away to each other like little swallows.

He got off at Gokuraku-ji. He wasn't sure of the exact address but, in a small valley town like this, it wouldn't be hard to find the house in question, if indeed it even existed.

Mihara went to the local police box, identified himself to the young officer on duty and asked whether there was a Yasuda living in the area.

'Ah, you mean the lady who's unwell?' said the officer. Mihara felt a strange twang of disappointment. Yasuda had been telling the truth.

Well, he was here now. Mihara set off in the direction the officer had indicated, the box of cakes dangling at his side.

It was a quiet neighbourhood. Some of the houses had straw-thatched roofs. On one side rose the mountains; on the other, beyond the houses, Mihara could glimpse the sea.

9. Landscape with Figures

I

The house stood at the bottom of a gentle slope, quite far from the station. Most of the houses in the neighbourhood were ringed with bamboo fences or cedar hedges. Patches of blue sea were visible between them. The Yasuda residence, a cosy-looking one-storey building with a thick hedge, looked exactly like the kind of home in which one might find a convalescing wife.

Mihara pushed the doorbell and heard a buzzer ring in the house. He instinctively steadied his breathing. These sorts of visits were always tricky.

An elderly housemaid opened the door.

'My name is Mihara. I've come from Tokyo. I'm fortunate enough to know Mr Yasuda, and as I was in the area I thought I'd drop by and see how his wife is getting on.'

The maid listened politely, her head bowed, then went to announce him. Soon she reappeared, knelt in the doorway, and said, 'Please, come in.'

Mihara was shown to a Japanese-style room at the back of the house, perhaps eight tatami mats in size. The bright sunshine of early spring flooded in through a south-facing sliding glass door and reached the middle of the room, where it bathed the sheets of a futon bed a dazzling white.

A pale young woman was sitting up in the bed, awaiting her visitor. The maid began arranging a haori on her shoulders. The jacket's dark and lustrous silk, speckled with red, threw the woman into sharp relief against the bedsheets. She was probably in her early thirties. Her hair was tied loosely at the back, and her slender face bore a light layer of make-up that must have been hastily applied in anticipation of her visitor.

'My apologies for dropping in on you like this,' he began. 'Let me introduce myself. My name is Mihara. I've had the pleasure of meeting your husband in Tokyo. I happened to be in the neighbourhood and felt I should pay you a visit.' Of course, he couldn't very well hand her his card, bearing as it did the crest of the Tokyo Metropolitan Police.

'Not at all. Thank you very much for stopping by. I'm sure my husband is lucky to know you.'

Yasuda's wife was very beautiful, with large eyes and a long, slender nose. Though there was a certain sharpness to her jawline, her illness did not seem to have marked her too severely. Her pale, slightly gaunt face and broad forehead gave her an intelligent air.

'How are you feeling?' asked Mihara. He was beginning to feel guilty for deceiving her.

'Thank you for asking. It's a long-term condition, so I've given up any hope of a sudden recovery,' she said, a vague smile playing about her thin lips.

'I'm sorry to hear that. But I suppose the warmer weather will do you some good. It's been a harsh winter this year.'

'The winters are milder here,' she replied, squinting slightly in the bright light. 'Around three degrees warmer than Tokyo, I'm told. But I feel the cold all the same. I'm certainly glad spring is on the way.'

She looked up at Mihara, almost imploringly. She had bright, beautiful eyes, although something in her gaze suggested she was fully aware of their effect. 'If I might ask, do you know my husband through business?'

'Yes, in a way,' replied Mihara vaguely. This was excruciating. He would have to explain himself to Yasuda later.

'I see. Then I suppose he must owe you all sorts of favours.'

'No, no – quite the opposite,' said Mihara, a light sweat forming on his brow. 'So, is your husband able to visit often?' he asked, hurriedly changing the subject.

Yasuda's wife smiled serenely. 'He's a busy man, but he still manages to come once a week.' This tallied with what Yasuda had told him.

'I suppose being busy is a good thing. Must be difficult for you, though.'

As he spoke, Mihara glanced discreetly around the room. Her illness must have left her with plenty of time on her hands, he thought, noting the stacks of books by the traditional alcove. On top of one was a literary monthly. This surprised him slightly – he would have expected something lighter. Atop another pile was a foreign novel in translation, underneath which were several copies of what looked like a small magazine, the same thickness as the novel. As the covers were obscured, Mihara couldn't see what the publication was.

The maid brought some tea, but Mihara, feeling it was time to leave, made to get up.

'Sorry again for surprising you like this. Please – do look after yourself.'

Yasuda's wife looked up at him, and her eyes, almost blue in the light, seemed to sparkle. 'Thank you very much for visiting.'

When he presented her with the box of cakes, she bowed politely from her bed, and Mihara noticed for the first time how frail her shoulders were.

The maid saw him to the door. As Mihara was putting on his shoes, he asked in a low, discreet voice, 'Who is her doctor?'

The elderly woman smiled and replied immediately. 'Dr Hasegawa. His clinic is near Daibutsu-mae.'

2

Mihara took the Enoshima line to Daibutsu-mae. Ranks of excited schoolchildren were still streaming about. It didn't take him long to find Dr Hasegawa's clinic. Here, at least, he didn't hesitate to hand over his card.

Dr Hasegawa was a stout man with ruddy cheeks, narrow eyes and grey, neatly combed hair. He set Mihara's card on the desk, then looked up at him.

'I'd like to ask you a few questions about Mrs Yasuda's condition,' said Mihara. Dr Hasegawa glanced at the card again before turning his gaze back to Mihara.

'Are you here in an official capacity?'

'Yes.'

'And does your query concern her personal life?'

'No, nothing like that. I'd just like to know a little about her condition. A simple explanation will be fine.'

The doctor nodded, then asked a nurse to bring Mrs Yasuda's medical records.

'Mrs Yasuda has disseminated tuberculosis. It's a long-term condition, quite troublesome to treat. She's been ill for three years already. To put it bluntly, the chances of a full recovery are looking slim. I've told Mr Yasuda. Right now, I'm just keeping her strength up with injections of a recently developed drug.'

'So she's bedridden?'

'She can get up from time to time. But she gets very tired if she's on her feet too long.'

'Does that mean she can't leave the house?' asked Mihara.

'No, she's able to go on short walks. Sometimes she even stays with her family in Yugawara for a night or two. That much she can manage.'

'And do you visit her every day?'

'No, not every day. Her condition isn't likely to suddenly deteriorate, so I just check up on her on Tuesdays and Fridays. Oh, and I sometimes drop by on Sunday afternoons, too.'

Noticing Mihara's intrigued expression, the doctor smiled slightly. 'She has literary tastes, you see. Patients in her situation often turn to waka or haiku, but she reads novels too. She even writes her own short pieces from time to time.'

Mihara recalled the foreign novels and literary magazines he'd seen in her room.

'In fact, I dabble in literature myself. I used to be acquainted with the writer Masao Kume. These days, there are all sorts of literary types living here in Kamakura, but Mr Kume was my one and only brush with that world. I'm a little too old for all that now. But I am a member of a small literary circle – a group of people my age who write essays or poetry. Together we put out a small quarterly magazine. It's just a hobby, really – a bit like cultivating bonsai or something. Anyway, Mrs Yasuda has similar interests, so I sometimes visit her on Sunday afternoons and we have a little chat. She seems to enjoy it as much as I do. Six months ago, she even gave me the manuscript of an essay she'd written.'

The doctor, warming to his subject now, offered to show Mihara the issue of the magazine where Mrs Yasuda's essay had been published.

'Here we are,' he said, bringing over a magazine of around thirty pages whose cover bore the title *Nanrin*. Mihara scanned the table of contents and turned to the relevant page.

Under the mysterious heading 'Landscape with Figures', he saw the words 'Ryōko Yasuda'. So that was her name: Ryōko. Mihara began to read.

Bedridden for too long, one gets the urge to read all sorts of books. Lately, however, I have grown weary of novels. Often I will read only a third of the way through before losing interest and setting the book to one side. One day, my husband came to visit me and happened to leave his train timetable behind. I ended up flicking through it, purely out of boredom. Now, there I was, stuck in bed with no prospect of travelling whatsoever, and yet I found this timetable quite absorbing – certainly far more so than any second-rate novel. My husband always buys a copy of the timetable and refers to it often on his business trips. Here on my sickbed, I have found in it an entirely less practical kind of pleasure.

The timetable contains the names of all the stations in Japan. As I read them, I imagine not only the station but also the surrounding landscape. Toyotsu, Saikawa, Sakiyama, Yusubaru, Magarikane, Ita, Gotōji: these are the names of the stations on a rural train line in Kyushu. Shinjō, Masukata, Tsuya, Furukuchi, Takaya, Karikawa, Amarume: a branch line in Tohoku. Yusubaru, for example, brings to my mind a village nestled in the mountains where lush southern trees grow. Amarume, on the other hand, suggests a desolate Tohoku townscape, grey sky looming overhead. I can picture to myself the mountains surrounding those villages and towns, the way the houses look, even the people walking to and fro. In his famous *Essays on Idleness*, Kenkō writes: 'As soon as I hear someone's name, I feel I can picture their face.' My mind works in much the same way. Whenever I find myself at a loose end, I can open the timetable at any page and enjoy travelling through San'in, Shikoku or Hokuriku – wherever I please.

More recently, my imagination has begun to travel not only in space but also in time. For example, I glance at my watch and see that it is 1.36 in the afternoon. Then I skim through the timetable, looking for a station accompanied by the numbers 13.36. I discover that, at this very point in time, train number 122 is arriving at a station named Sekiya on the Echigo line. At Akune, on the Kagoshima main line, passengers are disembarking from train number 139. Train number 815 is just pulling in to Hidamiyata. In Fujiu on the Sanyō line, Iida in Shinshū, Kusano on the Jōban line, Higashinoshiro on the Ōu main line, Ōji on the Kansai main line – at each of these stations, a train has just reached the platform.

At the very moment that I lie in bed, contemplating my emaciated fingers, trains are simultaneously coming to a halt all across the country. Countless people are getting on and off them, each following the course of their own life. I close my eyes and imagine these scenes. I am even able to work out, for each line, the stations at which trains are passing each other at that particular moment. This brings me great pleasure. The crossing of the trains is inevitable in time, but the meeting of their passengers in space is entirely accidental. I can fantasize endlessly about the lives led by all these people who, in faraway places, are brushing past each other at this very moment. I derive far more enjoyment from these flights of fancy than from any novel produced by someone else's imagination. Mine is the solitary, wandering pleasure of dreams.

Yes – these days, the railway timetable, with its dense rows of numbers and unfamiliar names, has become my favourite reading material.

'Intriguing idea, isn't it?' observed the doctor, once Mihara had finished reading. His eyes narrowed even further as he smiled. 'I suppose her mind has plenty of time to wander.'

'Yes, I'm sure . . .' replied Mihara absent-mindedly as he handed back the magazine. He had briefly forgotten the doctor's existence, though this owed less to Ryōko Yasuda's sensibility and more to a single sentence found towards the beginning of the essay: 'My husband always buys a copy of the timetable and refers to it often on his business trips.'

3

It was almost eight o'clock in the evening when Mihara got back to his office. Inspector Kasai had already left for the night.

On Mihara's desk, under an ink bottle, was a telegram. That was fast, he thought, then opened it before even sitting down. As expected, it was from the Sapporo Police up in Hokkaido, responding to his enquiry.

> Kawanishi of the Futaba company says he met
> Yasuda at Sapporo station on 21 Jan.
> Yasuda stayed at Marusō inn from 21 to 24 Jan.

Mihara had half expected this reply, but it left him disappointed all the same.

So Kawanishi did meet him at the station, and he did stay at the Marusō. It was all just as Yasuda had said.

Mihara sat down and lit a cigarette. There was no one else in the office. This was good: he had some thinking to do.

Yes, the response had been just as he'd expected. Nothing in it contradicted Yasuda's account. Of course it didn't: Yasuda wasn't stupid enough to tell such a blatant lie. So he really had arrived in Hokkaido on the twenty-first.

Sayama and Toki had committed suicide, all the way down in Kyushu, on the night of the twentieth; their bodies had been found the following morning. At that time, Yasuda must have been en route to Hokkaido on the Towada Express. Otherwise, he could not have met Kawanishi at Sapporo station.

But Mihara couldn't stop thinking about Yasuda's ingenious use of that four-minute window at Tokyo station. He had created witnesses to Sayama and Toki's departure, though his underlying purpose for doing so was still unclear. And precisely because it was unclear, Mihara couldn't help connecting Yasuda with the suicide that had taken place in Kyushu between the twentieth and the twenty-first. He knew he was being obstinate in clinging so fiercely to this idea. The problem now was that Yasuda had travelled in the opposite direction to Kyushu: instead of going south, he had gone north!

Wait, thought Mihara. Isn't it odd that he travelled in the *exact* opposite direction?

He lit a second cigarette. Something told him Yasuda's direction of travel had not been an accident. No – like the four-minute interval at the station, it had the whiff of a stratagem.

Mihara had an idea. He opened a drawer and took out the file containing the reports on the suicides. It had been Torigai of the Fukuoka Police who had so carefully assembled this file for him, and now he thought, for the first time in a while, of that detective with the thin cheeks and wrinkled eyes.

The autopsy report stated that Sayama and Toki had died from cyanide poisoning, between 10 and 11 p.m. on the twentieth of January. The verdict was double suicide.

Mihara fetched the railway timetable that was kept in the office and thumbed through it. At the time of the deaths, he noted, the Towada Express had been running along the Jōban line from Nakoso, famous for its ancient ruins, past Taira, and was somewhere in the vicinity of Hisanohama and Hirono. Then he checked the time when the bodies had been discovered, around 6.30 a.m. on the twenty-first, and saw that the train would have just left Ichinohe station in Iwate prefecture. If Yasuda had been on that train, then he was completely separated in both time and space from everything that had happened on Kashii beach.

Mihara smiled wryly to himself as he realized he was starting to view the timetable in just the manner described by Ryōko Yasuda in her essay. She had written that Yasuda was always consulting the railway timetable. Did that perhaps mean he knew its secrets? In any case, his familiarity with the train times had to signify something. What if Yasuda's entire alibi was built on it?

But 'alibi' wasn't quite right. Yasuda's story merely established that he hadn't been in Tokyo. To really speak of an alibi, they needed to know that he hadn't gone to Kyushu in the meantime.

Mihara read the telegram again, then began twiddling it between his fingers. It wasn't that he didn't trust the statements it contained. He was sure the basic facts were indeed as claimed. But he also felt as though he were gazing up at the smooth surface of an edifice that concealed, somewhere in its depths, a more devious truth.

I need to visit Hokkaido, he thought.

If he was going to discover the flaw in the edifice, he would need to sound out its walls himself. Mihara vowed to himself that he would inspect every inch of that facade until he found a crack.

The next morning, when Inspector Kasai arrived, Mihara went straight over to his desk.

'The reply came from Sapporo,' he said, handing the telegram to Kasai, who cast an eye over it.

'Yasuda's story checks out, then,' said Kasai, looking back up at Mihara.

'Yes, but . . .'

'Take a seat. What is it?' Kasai had sensed Mihara had more to say.

'Actually, I went to Kamakura yesterday, while you were out.'

'Ah, yes. I saw your note.'

'I dropped in on Yasuda's wife. I wanted to see if he'd been telling us the truth about her. But there she was, in bed with tuberculosis, just as he'd said.'

'It would appear we can take the man at his word, then.'

'Well, yes, so far. But there was something else.'

Mihara told him about the essay by Ryōko Yasuda the doctor had shown him and how it hinted at Yasuda's intimate knowledge of the railway timetable.

'That *is* interesting,' said Kasai, clasping his hands together on the desk. 'Could explain his use of that four-minute interval at Tokyo station.'

'My thoughts exactly,' said Mihara, encouraged by the way Kasai had leaned forward to listen. 'His creation of witnesses at the station suggests strongly to me that he had something to do with Sayama and Toki's suicide. Now, this is all still a hunch. I don't have any hard evidence yet. But he was involved in some way, I can tell you that much.'

In other words, Mihara was convinced that the double suicide had been the smokescreen for a crime.

'Yes, I'd have to agree,' said Kasai, who had already come round to this view.

'I'd like your permission to go to Hokkaido. Somehow, I just don't buy the idea that Yasuda was really on his way there on the night of the suicides. I know we have the report from the Sapporo Police, but I feel that the facts are hiding something. Once we work out what that is, we'll know why Yasuda needed a third party to witness Sayama and Toki leaving Tokyo.'

Kasai did not reply immediately, instead looking away pensively. Then, all of a sudden, he said, 'Well, we've come this far! I want you to see this through to the end. I'll talk to the section chief.'

Sensing a change in Kasai's tone, Mihara glanced at him. 'Why, did he say we should drop the investigation?'

'Not exactly,' replied Kasai. 'He just doesn't see why we'd want to investigate such a clear case of double suicide. So no, he's not exactly enthusiastic about the idea. But don't worry,' he continued, flashing Mihara a reassuring smile. 'I'll talk him into it.'

10. The Hokkaido Witness

I

The next evening, Mihara set off from Ueno station on the Towada Express.

It was the same train Yasuda claimed to have taken. For Mihara, this wasn't just the most convenient way of reaching Hokkaido: he also wanted to retrace Yasuda's journey.

He fell asleep somewhere after Taira. The two people sitting in front of him had been chattering away in Tohoku dialect, and for a while their loud voices kept his nerves on edge. But at around 11 p.m. the day's work finally caught up with him and he found himself dozing off. Apart from briefly waking in Sendai when the carriage became noisy for a while, he slept until the train pulled into Asamushi, the second-to-last stop.

The sea looked fresh in the pale dawn light. On the train, people were preparing to disembark.

The guard came in and, standing in the entrance, wished the passengers a good morning. 'We will shortly be arriving in Aomori, our final stop. Thank you for travelling with us. All passengers wishing to take the Seikan ferry to Hakodate, please fill out a passenger form. I will be handing out the forms now,' he said, and began distributing them to passengers who raised their hand for one.

This was Mihara's first crossing to the northern island of Hokkaido. He took one of the forms. It was a single sheet of paper divided into two sections, A and B, in each of which, for some reason, he had to write his details. He handed his form in at the ticket gate.

They had arrived in Aomori at 9.09. It was forty-one minutes until the ferry departed, but people still dashed frantically down the long platform, anxious to secure a good seat. Mihara was jostled several times as they passed.

The ferry reached Hakodate at 2.20 in the afternoon. Thirty minutes later, the Marimo Express left for Sapporo, the island's capital. The trains and the ferry formed a seamless chain of connections.

For the next five and a half hours, Mihara had his first glimpses of Hokkaido from the train, but by now all he wanted was to get to Sapporo. When he arrived at the station that evening, he was on his last legs. Yasuda had probably made the journey from Ueno in comfort, travelling in a sleeper or at least a second-class carriage. Mihara, on his paltry detective's budget, could not afford the same luxury, and as a result his bottom ached.

He checked in at the cheapest inn he could find near the station. If he had stayed at the Marusō, it would have been easier to investigate Yasuda's movements, but that was another expense he couldn't afford.

That night, it began to rain. Mihara listened to the pitter-patter outside, his mind blank with exhaustion, then fell into a deep sleep.

It was just after ten in the morning when he woke with a start. The rain had stopped, and sunlight was pouring on to the tatami. It was a little chilly. Well, that's Hokkaido for you, he thought.

Mihara ate breakfast and then visited the Sapporo police station as a matter of courtesy. He greeted them and thanked them for their recent investigation.

'Did we miss something?' The chief inspector seemed anxious about the fact that someone had come all the way from Tokyo. Mihara assured him that everything in the report had been in order and he was here on a separate, personal investigation.

When he added that he was heading to the Marusō inn, the chief assigned a detective to show him the way. Mihara, thinking this would be helpful, didn't object.

Things went smoothly at the inn; they had already helped with the initial investigation. A maid appeared and immediately showed him the section of the guest register where Yasuda had written his name.

'He arrived on the evening of the twenty-first of January, at around nine o'clock,' she explained. 'He stayed here three nights, until the twenty-fourth. He was out on business during the day and came back early in the evening. I wouldn't say there was anything unusual about him. He was a quiet man.'

She gave a physical description of the guest, which matched Yasuda's appearance. Mihara asked to keep the register for reference, just in case. After leaving the inn, he dismissed the other detective. He would work alone from here.

The Futaba company occupied a large shop on the main street which sold machinery and equipment. The display windows were filled with motors and other gear.

Kawanishi was a man of around fifty with a receding hairline. He explained to Mihara that he was the company's sales manager. His eyes widened when he saw Mihara's police ID.

'Just the other day, a detective from the Sapporo Police came to ask me whether I had met Mr Yasuda at the station! Is he suspected of something?' Kawanishi looked completely taken aback.

'No, it's nothing like that. I'm just gathering information in relation to another matter. There's no cause for concern. Have you been in business with Mr Yasuda long?' asked Mihara, in a reassuring tone.

'Five or six years. He's a good man. Trustworthy, honest.'

Mihara gave a series of approving nods. 'So when Mr Yasuda arrived in Sapporo on the twenty-first of January, you met him at the station?'

This was the crucial question he had travelled all the way to Hokkaido to ask.

2

'That's right,' replied Kawanishi. 'He sent a telegram saying he was arriving on the Marimo on the twenty-first, and could I meet him in the waiting room at the station. I did as he asked. I'm afraid I didn't keep the telegram.'

'Do you always meet him at the station when he visits?' asked Mihara.

'No, not always. But as it was the evening, the shop was closed, and he said he had urgent business to discuss, so we ended up meeting at the station.'

'I see. So, when the Marimo arrived, did Mr Yasuda come and find you in the waiting room right away?'

Kawanishi seemed to mull the question over. 'Hmm, not exactly. The express gets in at 8.34. From the waiting room, I could see the disembarking passengers all going through the ticket gate and streaming out of the station, so I remember thinking he'd be along any moment, but in the end it was a good ten minutes before he got there.'

A short delay didn't seem significant. The fact remained that Yasuda must indeed have arrived on the Marimo.

Mihara was disappointed. He'd expected an answer like this, and yet he still felt bitter about the outcome. Ridiculous though it seemed, he had half a mind to ask Kawanishi if he was sure the man in question had really been Tatsuo Yasuda.

But no, there wasn't a sliver of doubt. Just as he had claimed, Yasuda had arrived in Sapporo by express train at 8.34 on the twenty-first and stayed at the Marusō until the twenty-fourth. Mihara felt like he was staring at a brick wall.

All his efforts had been futile, and now he wondered how he would ever apologize to Inspector Kasai, who had so generously supported him. When the section chief was unimpressed by the idea, Kasai had been the one to talk him into it. Mihara couldn't help but feel responsible.

He must have looked very downcast because, after some hesitation, Kawanishi said in a low voice:

'Inspector . . . Mihara, wasn't it? I'm not sure if Mr Yasuda would want me telling you this, but you've come all the way from Tokyo, so – well, there is one thing I noticed. But I must stress that this is simply an observation on my part. I'd rather you didn't read too much into it.'

'Of course. What is it?' asked Mihara, looking up at Kawanishi.

'Just now I mentioned that, in his telegram, Mr Yasuda said he was visiting on urgent business. But when we met, the matter didn't seem particularly pressing.'

'Oh?' asked Mihara. He felt a lump in his throat.

'Yes. It could definitely have waited until the next day, when the shop was open. I did find it a little odd at the time.'

Mihara felt as though a crack had suddenly opened in the wall that had been blocking his path. Still, though his heart was pounding with excitement, he maintained a calm exterior. In a quiet voice, he asked Kawanishi to repeat what he had just told him.

Yasuda had asked Kawanishi to meet him at the station, when in reality there was nothing urgent for them to discuss. Why?

Maybe, thought Mihara, Yasuda needed an eyewitness who would confirm that he had arrived at Sapporo station on the Marimo on the twenty-first of January. And maybe he had chosen Kawanishi.

That had to be it! There could be no other reason. It was just like the trick Yasuda had pulled at Tokyo station with the four-minute interval. In both cases, the witnesses were there not by chance but by design.

And if this were true, it cast doubt on Yasuda's claim that he had arrived on the Marimo. Mihara could even assume the opposite to be true. In short, perhaps Yasuda had never been on the train in the first place.

Then Mihara remembered what Kawanishi had told him earlier. There was a twinkle of excitement in his eyes now.

'Mr Kawanishi, you met Mr Yasuda in the waiting room, correct?'

'That's right.' Kawanishi looked like he was beginning to regret his moment of candour.

'You didn't meet him on the platform.'

'No, the telegram said I should meet him in the waiting room.'

'Which means,' said Mihara, cutting to the chase now, 'you didn't actually see Mr Yasuda getting off the train?'

'Well, no. But . . .'

But, Kawanishi seemed to want to say, *Mr Yasuda was coming from*

Tokyo, and he appeared in the waiting room at that time, so he must have got off that train.

Mihara left the shop abruptly, barely even aware of how he took his leave of Kawanishi. He began wandering the streets of Sapporo. It was his first time in the city, but he hardly noticed its wide avenues lined with tall acacia trees. Instead, as he roamed, his mind pursued a single thought.

Yasuda was lying. He had pretended to arrive on the Marimo and then, having summoned Kawanishi by telegram, met him in the waiting room of Sapporo station at the appropriate time. Kawanishi had indeed 'met him' at the station, just as the telegram from the Sapporo Police had claimed. Of course, anyone would assume Yasuda's appearance at the station meant he had arrived on the train. He knew this and had used it to his advantage.

At Tokyo station, Yasuda had made the two waitresses from the Koyuki his witnesses. In Hokkaido, it had been Kawanishi.

All right, Yasuda, he thought. I'm on to you now.

Mihara checked his notebook. Yasuda had stated the following:

Departed Ueno, Tokyo on 20 January (Towada Express), arrived Aomori on morning of 21 January, took the 9.50 ferry and arrived in Hakodate at 2.20 p.m. From Hakodate, travelled on the Marimo Express, which arrived in Sapporo at 8.34 p.m.

Looking at this schedule, Mihara almost gasped.

Of course! Why hadn't he thought of it earlier?

On the Seikan ferry, each passenger was required to fill out a form. If Yasuda had really been on board, he would be on that list. All he had to do was check the forms and surely Yasuda's story would crumble!

3

But Mihara's excitement soon turned to anxiety. The twenty-first of January was more than a month ago. Would they still have the passenger forms? If they had already been destroyed, then this crucial lead would have been lost with them.

They would be able to tell him at Sapporo station. He hurried there, breathless now, and found the office of the railway police. He introduced himself and asked how long the passenger forms were kept.

'For the Seikan ferry?' said the middle-aged officer on duty, wiping his face with his hand. 'They keep them for six months.'

Six months was plenty, thought Mihara with relief.

'And I assume the forms are kept at Aomori station?' he asked.

'Did the passenger in question get on at Aomori?'

'Yes.'

'Then you don't need to go all that way. They should have a copy at Hakodate.' Seeing Mihara's puzzled expression, the officer continued: 'The passenger forms have two identical sections, A and B. They separate them at the station. Section A is kept at the station of departure, while B is taken by the ship's captain and handed over to the station of arrival. In this case, they'll have a copy in Hakodate.'

'I see,' said Mihara. He remembered writing out his details on both sections of the form.

'Which date are you interested in?' asked the officer.

'The twenty-first of January. It's the ferry that arrived at Hakodate at 2.20.'

'That'll be the No. 17. If you want, I can call Hakodate and ask them to get the forms ready for you.'

'I'd be very grateful if you could. Tell them I'll take the night train and be there in the morning.'

Mihara left the office. His train wouldn't depart until 10 p.m. that evening. That was eight hours away, and then it would be another eight hours to Hakodate. He was desperate to check those forms, and yet sixteen long hours stood obstinately in the way. He wandered aimlessly around Sapporo to kill the time but felt so jittery that his eyes scarcely took in the city's sights.

Finally, dusk fell. Then, after a train journey that felt like it would never end, passing slowly in a mix of agitation and sleep, Mihara arrived at Hakodate station just after six o'clock in the morning.

A cold wind was blowing. Mihara waited impatiently for another two hours until the station attendant appeared. Finally, he explained to the young man on duty what he had come for.

'Yes, they telephoned yesterday. I've already found the forms in question. The No. 17 on the twenty-first of January, wasn't it?' said the attendant, dumping two bundles of forms, tied together with string, on to the table. 'They're divided into second and third class. Which one would you like?'

'Second, I think, though there's a chance it could be third,' replied Mihara. The third-class bundle was far bigger than the second-class one and looked like it would take some time to sift through.

· 'These are the second-class ones.'

There must have been fewer than thirty forms. Mihara began working his way through them in order. Yasuda's name won't be here, there's no way it could be here, Mihara kept saying to himself. When he reached the twelfth or thirteenth form, he paused, his eyes drawn to these words:

Yoshio Ishida, government official, age 50, Tokyo, —

Yoshio Ishida was the division chief at Ministry X. Mihara knew him only too well: he was at the centre of the bribery scandal that the Second Division was so focused on investigating.

So Ishida had come to Hokkaido on the ferry. Mihara was beginning to feel uneasy. He carried on carefully leafing through another five or so forms – before almost crying out, despite himself.

There he was!

Tatsuo Yasuda, machinery dealer, age 42, Tokyo, —

His eyes scanned the words. He couldn't believe it. It wasn't possible, and yet the cold truth lay there before him, as if in close-up.

Mihara could scarcely breathe. With trembling fingers, he took the guest register he had confiscated from the Marusō inn out of his bag and placed Yasuda's entry alongside the form. As if to rub salt in Mihara's wound, the handwriting was a perfect match.

Yasuda had been on the ferry after all.

Mihara felt himself turning pale. Here was clear proof not only that Yasuda had travelled on the ferry, but also that he had boarded the connecting train, the Marimo. Every word of Yasuda's statement had been true.

That crack in the wall had been nothing but a mirage. Mihara felt crushed. He held his head in his hands and, for a moment, could only stare at the piece of paper in front of him.

11. An Unbreakable Barrier

I

Mihara walked out of the Tokyo Police headquarters and boarded a tram bound for Shinjuku. It was around eight o'clock in the evening, and the rush hour had subsided. The carriage was empty. He sat down slowly and, crossing his arms, felt a pleasant jolting sensation at his back as the tram moved off.

Mihara liked to ride the trams of Tokyo. Often, he would board without a specific destination in mind. Odd as it might seem, whenever he was at a loss for ideas, he would simply sit on the tram and allow his thoughts to roam. The tram's steady trundle, its gentle swaying, induced in him an almost euphoric state of contemplation. As the tram made its frequent stops, each time moving off again with a clatter, he relaxed further and further into his seat. And, having thus sealed himself off from the world, he could sink deep into thought.

Yasuda had sent Kawanishi a telegram asking to be met at Sapporo station, and yet he had nothing particularly urgent to discuss. In that case, why summon Kawanishi to meet him? Pondering this question, Mihara's expression turned vacant, and he scarcely registered the other passengers chattering away or getting on and off the tram.

Surely, he thought, Yasuda had asked Kawanishi to come to the station because he needed someone to confirm his arrival at Sapporo station on the Marimo. Kawanishi was the eyewitness who would support his alibi.

His alibi? Mihara puzzled over this word that had popped into his head. His alibi for what exactly? For not being *where*? Now Mihara was closing in on a truth he had previously only vaguely surmised. The only possible answer, of course, was Kashii beach. Yasuda's alibi was intended to prove that he hadn't been at the scene of the double suicide.

Mihara got out the timetable that had recently become a perm- anent fixture in his pocket. Assuming that Sayama and Toki had died between 10 and 11 p.m. on the twentieth of January, the next avail- able train from Hakata to Tokyo would have been the Satsuma, an express which left at 7.24 the following morning. But at 8.44 on the evening of the twenty-first, when Yasuda had met Kawanishi at Sap- poro station in Hokkaido, the Satsuma would have only just left Kyoto station.

This was what Yasuda had been trying to show: that he had not been present at the scene of the double suicide. But why go to such lengths to do so?

'Sir?' said the conductor, nudging Mihara's shoulder. The tram had already reached its last stop in Shinjuku. He disembarked and then, a little disoriented, walked down the brightly lit street before boarding another tram. This one was bound for Ogikubo.

Wait a moment, thought Mihara as he settled into his new seat. Maybe this wasn't the only time Yasuda had been trying to prove his absence. Those witnesses he'd created at Tokyo station might have served the same purpose. Until now, he'd assumed that Yasuda's sole aim had been to ensure the waitresses saw Sayama and Toki board- ing the train together. Now he realized there had been another reason: Yasuda wanted to make it clear that he himself had no pos- sible connection to the double suicide. By calling out 'Look! Isn't that Toki?' as the couple were boarding the train, he was showing Tomiko and Yaeko that he was simply a bystander – a witness just like them. The waitresses had even seen Sayama and Toki sitting on board the Asakaze. Yasuda, meanwhile, was on a separate train, bound for Kamakura. Here too, then, he had been establishing his alibi. He had even driven the point home by showing his face at the Koyuki the following two evenings.

There was no longer any doubt about it: these four-minute

witnesses existed not by chance but by design. Kawanishi in Sapporo, the waitresses in Tokyo: they were all witnesses of Yasuda's own creation. Their purpose was to prove that he could not possibly have been at the scene of the double suicide.

In the end, though, Yasuda's actions in Sapporo and Tokyo pointed to only one place – the suburb of Kashii, outside Hakata, in Kyushu. Because everything Yasuda had done formed a single picture, one that said *I was not in Kashii that night*. Mihara felt increasingly confident that, in fact, that was precisely where he had been. The man's actions were so clearly deliberate that the picture they formed had to be false. And to discover the truth, all Mihara had to do was invert that picture.

Yes: on the twentieth of January, between 10 and 11 p.m., when Sayama and Toki committed suicide, Tatsuo Yasuda had, beyond a shadow of a doubt, been on that beach. And he had *done something*. What exactly that something was, Mihara didn't know. But he was sure Yasuda had been there that day. He must have watched as Sayama and Toki swallowed the poison and crumpled to the ground. All Yasuda's efforts were directed at forming a picture that was the exact opposite of this scenario.

This, it seemed to Mihara, was the only logical conclusion. But if it were true, Yasuda must have left Hakata at 7.24 the following morning on the Satsuma Express bound for Tokyo. By 8.44 that evening, the Satsuma was only just leaving Kyoto station – and yet that was when Yasuda had met Kawanishi at Sapporo station, a smile on his face. It seemed unlikely that Kawanishi had been lying. In any case, it was certain that Yasuda had strolled into the Marusō inn at around 9 p.m. At that time, the Satsuma Express would still have been travelling along the shore of Lake Biwa, just east of Kyoto. What to make of this discrepancy between logic and reality?

This wasn't all. There was also the passenger form for the Seikan ferry, a seemingly irrefutable piece of evidence supporting Yasuda's statement. That alone was enough to dismantle Mihara's theory entirely.

But he did not lose heart. Propelling him forward, against the odds, was an instinctive distrust of Yasuda that no amount of apparent evidence to the contrary could shake.

'Excuse me!' It was the conductor. The tram had reached Ogikubo and the other passengers had all disembarked. Mihara got off and changed to a local train line that would take him back towards Ginza.

Yasuda had built his edifice carefully. The construction looked solid, but there had to be a weak point. The question was, where?

Mihara continued his thoughts, his eyes half closed now, a breeze from the open window buffeting his face.

After about forty minutes, he suddenly looked up and found himself staring blankly at a cosmetics advertisement in the carriage. But the advertisement was irrelevant. Mihara had just remembered that one of the passenger forms at Hakodate station had borne the name of Yoshio Ishida, the division chief at Ministry X.

2

'I've dug up some more information on Ishida,' said Inspector Kasai.

Sending someone to question Ishida directly would have ruffled too many feathers, especially since the ongoing investigation already had the ministry on edge. Knowing this, Kasai had used subtler methods.

'He was indeed on a business trip to Hokkaido on the twentieth of January. He left Ueno station at 7.15 p.m. on the Towada and arrived in Sapporo on the Marimo at 8.34 the following evening. In other words, he travelled on exactly the same trains as Yasuda.'

The chief handed him a copy of Ishida's schedule for that day. It showed that, rather than leaving the train in Sapporo, he had travelled on to Kushiro. The rest of his trip had taken him to the various administrative divisions of Hokkaido.

'I had someone enquire discreetly about Yasuda. Ishida confirmed they were on the same train to Sapporo. Yasuda was also travelling second class, but they were in different carriages. Apparently, Yasuda dropped by to say hello from time to time, which is why Ishida is sure he was on board. He says he recognized Yasuda straight away because the two of them do business.'

'I see,' said Mihara, clearly disappointed. Here was another eye-witness asserting that Yasuda had been on that train. This time, it wasn't one of Yasuda's manufactured witnesses but a high-ranking ministry official whose business trip would have been scheduled several days in advance. His name had even been on the ferry register. There was simply no room for doubt.

'Mihara,' said Kasai, getting to his feet. He had noticed the inspector's downcast face. 'Looks like a nice day out there. How about we take a walk?'

Outside, it was indeed bright and sunny. With summer just around the corner, lots of passers-by were in short sleeves. The chief led the way, crossing the busy street to stand by the moat of the Imperial Palace. The white walls of the palace gleamed in the sun. After the darkness of the office, everything around them was so dazzling as to seem almost transparent. They strolled for a while, looking out over the moat, until the chief found a bench for the two of them to sit on. To those passing by, they must have simply looked like two office workers who had slipped out for a break.

'While you were away in Hokkaido, I had someone look into Sayama and Toki's relationship,' he said, taking out a pack of cigarettes and offering Mihara one.

Mihara couldn't help glancing at the chief. Sayama and Toki had gone as far as committing suicide together; surely they had been deeply in love. What could Kasai have hoped to gain from investigating their relationship?

'Pointless as that might seem,' said Kasai, as if reading Mihara's mind, 'I wanted to be sure. The thing is, they must have kept a very tight lid on their affair, because nobody had the faintest idea about them. Even the waitresses at the Koyuki were surprised to hear that Toki had chosen to end her life with Sayama. Women working in places like that are usually pretty good at sniffing things out, and yet none of them realized what was going on. Still' – and here the chief puffed on his cigarette, as if to signal that what he was about to say was important – 'it does seem certain that Toki had a lover. She lived alone in her small apartment, but she often received phone calls. The concierge who usually answered the phone said the caller was a woman who gave her name as Aoyama. Sometimes there was gramophone music in the background, so perhaps she was the proprietress of a coffee shop. But it seems she'd only been asked to call Toki for the sake of appearances, because the voice would always change to that of a man once Toki came to the phone. Whenever one of these calls came, Toki would bustle about, getting herself ready, and then head out. This had been going on for about six months before her death, but Toki never had any male visitors to her apartment. In other words, she seems to have been pretty careful about meeting her lover.'

'And the lover in question was Sayama?' asked Mihara. A vague doubt was beginning to form in the back of his mind.

'Presumably. I had him investigated, too, but he was even more of a mystery than Toki. Seems to have been a very quiet man – timid, too. Not the type to go around chatting about his love life. But the way he and Toki committed suicide makes it clear they were intimate.'

The chief sounded slightly unconvinced by his own assertion. Noticing this, Mihara's own feeling of apprehension seemed to intensify.

'Next, I had someone inquire into Yasuda's private life,' said Kasai, looking over at the pine trees in the palace grounds. The small figure of a guard could be seen standing at the top of the stone wall.

Mihara looked steadily at the chief. He realized that while he had been in Hokkaido invisible currents had been swirling around his superior, pushing him to act. Of course, even Kasai was just one cog in the wider machinery of the investigation.

'That didn't turn much up either,' murmured the chief, taking no heed of the troubled expression that had come over Mihara's face. 'Yasuda goes to see his sick wife in Kamakura once a week. It's possible he's been involved with other women, but we haven't uncovered any clear evidence. If he does have a mistress, he's kept her nicely hidden. Or maybe we've got him wrong and the man really is a devoted husband. I mean, as far as we can tell, he and his wife are certainly on good terms.'

Mihara nodded. This tallied with his own impression from his visit to Ryōko Yasuda in Kamakura.

'In other words, it seems all three of them – Toki, Sayama and Yasuda, if Yasuda even had a mistress – did a very good job of keeping their affairs secret.'

At these words, all Mihara's doubts seemed to coalesce into a single, precise form.

'Chief . . .' he said, his pulse quickening. 'Why all these new lines of enquiry? Has something changed?'

'Yes,' replied Kasai without a moment's hesitation. 'It's the superintendent. He seems to have become very interested in the double suicide all of a sudden.'

From this Mihara intuited that it wasn't just the superintendent who was interested; the pressure must have come from even higher up. And, as Kasai went on to explain, he was right.

3

The next day, when Mihara returned to the office, Inspector Kasai called him over.

'Mihara, we've received a message from Division Chief Ishida.'

The chief had propped his elbows on his desk and clasped his hands together, which usually meant something was bothering him.

'No, he didn't visit us himself. His assistant dropped by. Ah yes – he left a card.'

The assistant's card read 'Kitarō Sasaki. Clerk, Ministry X'. Mihara glanced at it and waited for the chief to speak.

'Ishida says he recently received an enquiry from a certain gentleman about Tatsuo Yasuda. But he seems to have twigged that it was really the Tokyo Police asking, which is why he's sent us this message directly. He confirmed that he and Yasuda were on the same train to Hokkaido on the twentieth of January. He says they were in different carriages, but Yasuda dropped by to see him from time to time. If we need someone to corroborate this, we're to speak to a Hokkaido government official named Katsuzō Inamura, who was sitting with Ishida after the two of them happened to board the train together at Hakodate. At some point after the train had passed Otaru, Yasuda came to say goodbye because he was getting off at Sapporo, the next stop. Apparently, that was when Ishida introduced Inamura to him. Inamura should remember the encounter. That was the gist of Ishida's message.'

'Really sticking up for Yasuda, isn't he?' said Mihara.

'That's one way of looking at it. Though he probably just wants to show his willingness to cooperate with the police, seeing as he knows Yasuda is under investigation,' replied Kasai with a smile. Mihara knew what the smile meant.

'What's his relationship with Yasuda like?'

'Well, we're talking about a businessman and a government official – you know how that usually works. Plus, there's the fact that Ishida is a prime suspect in the bribery scandal. We haven't uncovered any shady deals between the two yet, but Yasuda has been doing plenty of business with the ministry, so I imagine he's been sending Ishida gifts on all the appropriate occasions. Going to all this trouble to defend Yasuda might well be Ishida's way of saying thank you.'

Kasai cracked his knuckles.

'But then, none of that makes much difference if he's telling the truth about the train. I did send a telegram with some questions for this Hokkaido official, just in case, but I'm sure his answers will match Ishida's statement. In other words, it looks like Yasuda really was on the Marimo on the twenty-first of January.'

Here was yet another witness confirming Yasuda's presence on the train. Mihara, exhausted, took his leave.

It was just past noon. Mihara went to the cafeteria on the fifth floor of the police headquarters. It was a large hall, about the size of a department store restaurant. Bright sunshine slanted through the windows. Mihara didn't feel like eating, and instead ordered some tea. He sat down, took a sip, then opened his notebook and wrote the following.

Yasuda's trip to Hokkaido:

1. Passenger form filled out in his name for the Seikan ferry. (No. 17. Connects with Marimo in Hakodate.)
2. Statement from Division Chief Ishida.
3. After the train had passed Otaru, Ishida introduced Yasuda to a Hokkaido government official.
4. Yasuda met Kawanishi at Sapporo station.

Mihara looked at what he had written and plunged into thought. These four points seemed like so many layers of unbreakable bedrock. And yet break them was exactly what he wanted to do. No – what he needed to do.

He could find no connection between the Satsuma, which left Hakata at 7.24 on the morning of the twenty-first, and the Marimo, which arrived in Sapporo at 8.34 in the evening of the same day. It was a puzzle with no solution. In other words, *there could be no connection*.

And yet it was an undeniable fact that Yasuda had appeared at Sapporo station.

Mihara, his head in his hands, must have read this list a dozen times before he noticed something strange.

Inamura, the Hokkaido official, met Yasuda after the train had passed Otaru station. Supposedly, Yasuda had stopped by their carriage to say goodbye to Ishida. But why hadn't he visited their carriage earlier?

Ishida, Inamura and Yasuda had all been on the same train from Hakodate, even if Yasuda was in a separate carriage. If, as Ishida claimed, Yasuda had been dropping by 'from time to time' to say hello, why had Inamura only met him after Otaru?

Mihara got out his train timetable and saw that it was a five-hour journey between Hakodate and Otaru on an express train. If Yasuda was on such good terms with Ishida, it seemed inconceivable that he had stayed in a separate carriage for five straight hours, as if they were perfect strangers. Come to think of it, why hadn't he taken a seat in Ishida's carriage? They could have whiled away the long journey in conversation. Even supposing he hadn't wanted to impose, it still seemed bizarre that he hadn't shown his face once during those five hours.

Strictly speaking, Inamura was the only impartial witness here. And he was the one who only saw Yasuda after Otaru . . .

Then a thought flashed through Mihara's mind.

What if Yasuda boarded the Marimo at Otaru?

This would explain why Inamura saw Yasuda only after the train had passed that station. It would also explain why Yasuda had been in a separate carriage: he didn't want them to see him boarding at Otaru. Then, once the train set off again, he could have strolled into the carriage, greeted Ishida and Inamura and, in so doing, convinced the latter that he had been on the train all the way from Hakodate.

It was as though the thick fog surrounding Mihara had finally been pierced by a faint light in the distance, revealing vague forms all around him. He felt almost giddy.

4

And yet it seemed impossible for Yasuda to have boarded the train at Otaru. In order to reach the station in time, he would have needed to leave Hakodate even earlier than the Marimo. From the perspective of the timetable, that seemed impossible.

But the idea that Yasuda had boarded the train at Otaru had taken hold of Mihara now. He had no idea how it was possible, but he sensed some hidden truth lurking behind these facts.

He took another sip of his tea, which was now quite cold, and left the cafeteria. His surroundings seemed indistinct, as if he were dreaming. He walked down the stairs in a daze.

Why would Yasuda have boarded the Marimo at Otaru? What was so important about that particular station? These questions looped around Mihara's mind like an endless refrain.

To board at Otaru he would have needed to travel on an earlier train than the Marimo. The previous train was the Akashiya, which left Hakodate at 11.39. Before that were two local trains and the first express train of the day, which left at six o'clock, but boarding any of those would have been an even more impossible feat.

Whatever it took, Mihara needed to place Yasuda at the scene of the double suicide in Kashii between ten and eleven o'clock on the evening of the twentieth of January. The precise reason could wait; for now all he cared about was pinning Yasuda to that location. But to get from Hakata all the way to Hokkaido, Yasuda's only option would have been the express to Tokyo at 7.24 on the morning of the twenty-first. The more Mihara thought, the more impossible it all seemed.

'Unless he had wings, there's simply no way he could have reached Hokkaido in time.'

As Mihara murmured these words to himself, he stumbled on the stairs – and not because they were poorly lit. He almost cried out in astonishment. Why hadn't he thought of this earlier?

His ears ringing, he dashed back to his office and, with trembling fingers, flicked to the back of the train timetable, where he found the schedule for Japan Airlines. He checked the flight times for January.

Fukuoka 08.00 → Tokyo 12.00 (Flight 302)
Tokyo 13.00 → Sapporo 16.00 (Flight 503)

'There it is!'

Mihara took a deep breath. There was still a buzzing in his ears.

Travelling by plane, Yasuda could have left Kyushu at eight o'clock in the morning and still have reached Sapporo at four o'clock in the afternoon. Mihara felt like slapping himself. How could he have forgotten the new passenger planes? He had been overly fixated on the trains, and the 7.24 Satsuma from Hakata had seemed like the only possibility. But now, at last, the fog had cleared.

Mihara called the airline and asked how long the bus from Chitose airport to downtown Sapporo took.

'Around an hour and twenty minutes. Then it's a ten-minute walk to the train station,' came the reply.

An hour and half after four o'clock: Yasuda could have reached Sapporo station by five thirty. The Marimo arrived only at 8.34 in the evening. What had Yasuda done during those three hours?

Mihara looked up the trains from Sapporo to Hakodate.

There was a local train that left Sapporo at 5.40. Sliding his finger down the page, he saw that it arrived at Otaru at 6.44. Then he checked the other direction. The Marimo, which left Hakodate at 2.50, arrived at Otaru at 7.51 – one hour and seven minutes after the train from Sapporo. Yasuda would have had a leisurely wait at Otaru station before boarding the Marimo and travelling back to Sapporo. He must have met Inamura soon after getting on the train.

Now it was clear why Yasuda had appeared in the carriage only after Otaru. Rather than wasting three hours in Sapporo, he had jumped off the airport bus and hurried to the station to catch the train to Otaru which left ten minutes later.

Yasuda had used these brief windows of time – ten minutes in Sapporo, and an hour and seven minutes in Otaru – to miraculous effect. Mihara was reminded of the four-minute interval at Tokyo station. He had to admit it: Yasuda was a genius at manipulating time.

Mihara went straight to Kasai's desk and, showing him the time-table, explained his discovery. His voice was trembling. When he had finished, Kasai looked steadily at him, his eyes gleaming with an excitement that could almost have been mistaken for anger.

'This is excellent work, Mihara!' he said. 'Simply excellent,' he repeated, the words seeming to tumble out uncontrollably. After a pause, he went on: 'So you've broken Yasuda's alibi. Wait – is it odd to call it an alibi?'

'No. Think about it: there's no longer anything stopping Yasuda from being at the scene of the suicide,' explained Mihara.

'Right. And if there's no reason he *couldn't* have been there . . .' began Kasai, drumming his fingers on the desk. 'Does that mean it's possible he *was* there?'

'I think it does,' said Mihara, a note of triumph in his voice.

'Well, now you need to prove it,' said the chief, looking directly at Mihara again.

'I can't, not just yet. Give me a little more time,' replied Mihara, looking worried again.

'Still a lot you need to clear up, isn't there?'

'Exactly.'

'For instance, you haven't cracked that alibi completely,' said Kasai, a troubled expression on his face. Mihara knew immediately what he was referring to.

'You mean Ishida.'

'Yes. Ishida.'

They met each other's gaze for a moment. It was Kasai who looked away and broke the silence.

'Don't worry. I'll take care of it.' The chief sounded elusive. Mihara sensed this was not the time to talk about Ishida. That could wait until later. Such was the wordless agreement that formed between them.

'Even setting that to one side, we still have a mountain to climb. What about Yasuda's passenger form on the ferry? That's more than just a witness statement: it's hard evidence.'

This was true. That form had been responsible for Mihara's crushing defeat at Hakodate station. Strangely, though, he no longer felt so disheartened. Yes, that sturdy-looking wall still blocked his path. But it no longer intimidated him.

'Don't you worry. I'll find a way.'

Kasai laughed for the first time. 'Raring to go, I see! You're a changed man from when you got back from Hokkaido. All right then – snap to it, Inspector.'

As Mihara made to leave, Kasai raised a hand to stop him. 'Funny, isn't it? Ishida went to all that trouble to cover for Yasuda, and now look where it's got him!'

5

Mihara was sure he had found the weak link in Yasuda's carefully constructed Marimo story. Now he just needed to prove it. He began jotting down his plan of attack:

Ask Japan Airlines for names of passengers who, on 21 Jan., booked both the 8 a.m. flight from Fukuoka to Tokyo and the connecting flight to Sapporo.

Wait a minute, thought Mihara. Yasuda's story was that he left Tokyo by the Towada Express at 7.15 on the evening of the twentieth. He would therefore have needed to stay in Tokyo until at least the afternoon of the twentieth. Knowing he would be investigated at some point, he wouldn't have been so careless as to be completely absent from Tokyo that day. He must have shown his face somewhere, perhaps at his office. But if he'd taken a train from Tokyo to Hakata in the afternoon, he'd never have made it to Kashii in time. Here, too, he must have travelled by plane.

Mihara checked the airline schedule again. The last flight from Tokyo to Fukuoka took off at 3.00 and landed at 7.20. It was a thirty-minute drive to Haneda. It would have seemed entirely reasonable for Yasuda to leave his office just after two o'clock, perhaps saying he had other business to attend to before his evening train from Ueno.

He decided to write down all the trains and planes he suspected Yasuda had taken.

20 January
3 p.m. dep. Tokyo Haneda → 7.20 p.m. arr. Fukuoka Itazuke
(Went to Kashii, then probably spent the night somewhere in Fukuoka)

21 January
8 a.m. dep. Itazuke → 12 p.m. arr. Haneda
1 p.m. dep. Haneda → 4 p.m. arr. Sapporo Chitose
5.40 p.m. dep. Sapporo (local train) → 6.44 p.m. arr. Otaru
7.57 p.m. dep. Otaru (Marimo Express) → 8.34 p.m. arr. Sapporo
(Met Kawanishi in waiting room of Sapporo station)

21–4 January
Stayed three nights at the Marusō inn in Sapporo, then returned to Tokyo.

There, thought Mihara. But as he scanned and re-scanned this itinerary, a question formed in his mind. Why, in his telegram, had Yasuda insisted that Kawanishi meet him in the waiting room? If

Yasuda had in fact boarded the Marimo at Otaru, why not tell Kawanishi to meet him on the platform and thus ensure he was seen actually leaving the train? Instead, he had specifically requested to be met in the waiting room. Yasuda was normally so meticulous that there had to be a reason. But, try as he might, Mihara couldn't work it out.

He would worry about that later. What he needed now was evidence of Yasuda's movements. He wrote down the following:

1. Check the Japan Airlines passenger lists for those days. (Also find out if anyone saw him taking the taxi to Haneda airport, or on the bus from the airport in Fukuoka or Sapporo – although the amount of time that has passed will make this difficult.)
2. Investigate the inns in Fukuoka where Yasuda may have stayed.
3. Find out if anyone saw Yasuda on the local train from Sapporo to Otaru, or at Otaru station, where he waited over an hour for the Marimo to arrive.

Mihara didn't hold out much hope for the third option. He decided it would probably come down to number one or two.

He gathered his things and left Tokyo Police headquarters. Outside, it was as just as bright as before. Ginza was full of people, the harsh sun bleaching their faces.

He walked into the Japan Airlines office and spoke to the domestic flights manager.

'Do you still have the passenger lists for January?'

'January of this year, I presume. Yes – we keep them for twelve months.'

'I need to know the name of a passenger who booked flight 305 to Fukuoka on the twentieth of January, as well as flight 302 to Tokyo and flight 503 to Sapporo on the twenty-first.'

'So all those bookings would be for the same person?'

'Yes.'

'Really getting around, weren't they! We don't get many people travelling like that, so this shouldn't take long.'

The employee brought out the airline's passenger records and turned to the twentieth of January. Flight 305 had made a stop in Osaka, with only forty-three passengers travelling all the way to Fukuoka. On the twenty-first, there had been forty-one people on the flight to Tokyo and fifty-nine on the flight to Sapporo. Tatsuo Yasuda's name was nowhere to be seen on the lists. Nor did any particular name occur more than once.

Mihara had expected Yasuda to travel under an alias, so it came as no surprise that his name wasn't here. But he was shocked by the fact that none of the one hundred and forty-three names on the lists matched any other. How was that possible?

'Can passengers travel without making a reservation?'

'Not usually. Even buying a ticket the day before can be difficult. You have to book three or four days in advance to be sure of a seat.'

These three planes formed an indispensable part of Yasuda's itinerary. Without them, he could never have connected with the Marimo on the twenty-first. He must have secured his seats personally, several days in advance. Even if he had used a fake name, it ought to appear on all three lists. But no matter how carefully Mihara looked, he found nothing.

'Thank you. Could I borrow these lists for a few days?'

Mihara wrote the clerk a receipt on one of his cards, then took the lists and left the office. He felt dejected; his earlier excitement had vanished. He walked to his usual café, where he sat with a coffee, pursued by his own thoughts. This can't be, he repeated to himself. It just wasn't possible.

He left the café and began making his way back to Tokyo Police headquarters. At the Hibiya intersection, he found himself waiting at the pedestrian crossing. Traffic streamed past. The signal was taking a long time to change. Mihara stared vacantly at the different vehicles driving past. Perhaps it was the very dreariness of the scene that spurred his thoughts, because just then, he let out a gasp.

What an idiot he'd been! Yasuda didn't need to use just *one* fake name. He could have booked his flights under a series of different aliases. Instead of visiting the Japan Airlines office in person, he must have sent a series of individuals to order his tickets. He could travel to Fukuoka as Mr A, back to Tokyo the next morning as Mr B, and then on to Sapporo as Mr C. With an hour between his flights at Haneda, he would have had plenty of time to board the next plane as a new passenger. It had been foolish to assume that just because Yasuda travelled on all three planes he would need to travel under a single name. Why hadn't he thought of this earlier? If he hadn't been in public, he would have slapped himself. I must be going soft in the head, he thought.

The signal turned green, and Mihara set off again.

Somewhere in these lists, he thought, there will be at least three fake names. Each will be a stand-in for Yasuda. We'll have the names and addresses on the lists checked: surely, three of them will turn out to be false.

Mihara looked up as he walked. For the first time, he felt that he could glimpse the path to victory.

6

Back at headquarters, Mihara reported to Kasai, who immediately agreed with his plan.

'Right then. A hundred and forty-three names, did you say?' he said, eyeing the lists. 'More than half from the Tokyo area, and the rest in the country . . . For the ones in Tokyo, we'll send our own detectives. For the others, we can ask the local police to make enquiries.

These arrangements were immediately put into action. The detectives scribbled down their assigned names and addresses in their notebooks.

'If they have a phone at their home or office, call them. The main thing is to make sure they were on that plane!'

Next, Kasai turned to Mihara. 'Even if this works, we're not out of the woods yet.'

'Right. There are still the passenger forms for the ferry.'

That unbreakable barrier still hadn't moved an inch. It seemed to rear up imposingly, blocking Mihara's path. But now a doubt flitted through his mind. Wasn't it odd that with both the ferry and the planes, it was the passenger list causing the problem? What if this was just another illusion, and the apparent similarity was luring him into another misapprehension?

Noticing Mihara's troubled expression, Kasai asked: 'Something the matter?'

But Mihara changed the subject. 'What about our other problem?' he asked.

'You mean Ishida? Well, as it happens, I met with an investigator from the public prosecutor's office yesterday,' said Kasai in a low voice.

'The investigation's turning in circles, Mihara. Sayama's suicide has put a real spanner in the works. You see, assistants like him are the fixers of the workplace. They're the ones the division and section chiefs rely on to actually get stuff done. The higher-ups are too busy scrambling up the career ladder to ever learn much about practical matters, but if you're an assistant section chief, that's all you've ever done. You've learned all sorts over the years, like a seasoned craftsman. Of course, the trade-off is that your career hits a ceiling. All you can do is watch as younger, better-qualified university graduates leapfrog past you. You're resigned to your lot. You might be raging on the inside, of course, but you can't let that show if you want to work in government.'

Kasai took a sip of the tea that a detective had brought him.

'But say your superior takes a shine to you – now, that's exciting. Suddenly you're given a tantalizing glimpse of a world you'd long assumed was out of reach. Promotion is on the cards again. So you work hard, you do your best to please them. But what's motivating your superior? If they end up promoting you on the basis of your expertise, then wonderful. But if they're only taking you under their wing in order to use you, then the whole thing's a con. You see, no matter how much of a big shot they become, they'll always need a safe pair of hands. *That's* why they're showering you with attention – because merely ordering you about wouldn't be half as effective. Now, the assistants know all this, of course, but, out of a desire for advancement more than self-preservation, they do as they're told. I suppose that's human nature. In fact, these sorts of bonds are what hold these government offices together in the first place.'

The chief propped his elbows on the desk.

'It's the same in this case. Everything converges on Sayama. It seems he was quite the skilled operator. His suicide has blown a hole in the public prosecutor's investigation. In reality, it was Sayama who formed the invisible link between all the senior officials. He was the linchpin. With him gone, they're tearing their hair out at the prosecutor's office. He left a gap behind that seems to get wider and wider the more they investigate. Meanwhile, the higher-ups will be breathing a sigh of relief.'

'And I imagine Ishida is one of them?' asked Mihara.

'Oh, he'll be the most relieved of all! In any case, assistant chiefs tend to be dutiful subordinates – just the type who might commit suicide to save their ministry in its hour of need. Whenever there's a suicide in a major corruption case, it's always someone of Sayama's rank.'

'So you're saying his death fits the pattern?'

'Well, normally they commit suicide on their own, but in his case there was a woman. That's unusual. Puts a bit of a romantic spin on things, doesn't it?'

Kasai fell silent. Mihara knew what he was thinking but said nothing. He realized now that the public prosecutor, the superintendent in charge of the investigation, and Kasai himself were all on his side. This gave him courage.

Later that day, Mihara had another look through the file on Sayama and Toki's suicide. He combed through the crime-scene report, the autopsy results, the photographs and the witness statements, scrutinizing every detail. A man and a woman had drunk juice laced with cyanide; then they had died at each other's side. He had looked through these documents dozens of times. There were no new revelations to be found here.

And yet Yasuda had gone to such lengths to ensure there were witnesses to the couple's departure from Tokyo. More than anything, Mihara needed to work out what role he had played in all this.

Three days later the investigation into the aeroplane passengers was completed. There wasn't a single false name among them. Every passenger on the three lists was a real person, and all one hundred and forty-three of them had insisted there was no mistake: they had been on the plane.

Mihara was dumbfounded. Once again, he held his head in his hands and despaired.

12. The Letter from Jūtarō Torigai

I

Dear Inspector Mihara,

I must apologize for not writing sooner. Three months have passed since we met in Hakata, and I'm afraid I have been rather a poor correspondent. Thank you very much for your long letter, which was a pleasant surprise.

Time passes quickly. I first made your acquaintance at the beginning of the year, when a cold wind was still blowing in from the Genkai Sea, and yet here we are in mid-May, when merely walking in the sun is enough to make one break out in a sweat. The Dontaku festival, famous in these parts, was the same bustling affair it is every year and, as is customary, its conclusion marked the beginning of summer. I would like to take this opportunity to invite you, when you have the time, to visit Hakata and see the festival for yourself.

But I see from your letter that you are still grappling with this vexing case. Ashamed as I am of my own laziness in old age, I cannot help but admire your energetic devotion to the task at hand. Glumly, I contemplate my ageing body, so accustomed to provincial life, and wish I were only a little younger. But now I am rambling.

As you know, under the indifferent eyes of my superiors within the Fukuoka Police, I conducted a modest investigation into the double suicide of the man and woman found on

Kashii beach on the morning of the twenty-first of January. I was surprised and delighted in equal measure to learn that, in your capable hands, the case is turning out to be more important than I could ever have imagined.

Thank you very much for your detailed account of subsequent developments. Reading your letter, I imagined each of the numerous difficulties you must have encountered. You ask me if I have any counsel to give, but I fear I am too senile to offer any particularly clever ideas, and I can only express my utmost admiration for your unwavering commitment.

Of course, no detective worth their salt ever wants to abandon a case. It is in their nature to persevere against the odds. Perhaps you will find this a tedious and obvious remark, but I ask you to indulge this old man a moment.

You see, I have been with the force for twenty years. The number of cases I have worked on during that period astounds even me. Fortunately, my career has been a relatively untroubled one – and yet, I have left plenty of cases unsolved. Looking back, there are all sorts of things I wish I'd done differently. In every instance, however, it comes down to the fact that I just didn't persevere. I kick myself, thinking: *I could have cracked that case, if I had only stuck at it a little bit longer.* Sometimes all it takes is the tiniest extra push in exactly the right place.

In one particular case, which, even twenty years on, I am unable to forget, the decomposing body of an old woman was found in the Hirao suburb of Fukuoka. She was deemed to have been strangled because of the cord marks on her throat. Now, her body was found in May, but the police doctor ruled that more than three months had passed since her death. This was also assumed to be the case because the corpse was dressed for winter in a traditional padded jacket. However, the suspect I'd identified had moved from Taiwan to the vicinity of the victim's house only at the beginning of April. In other words, he had been out of the country during the cold months of January, February and early March, when the victim would normally have worn a jacket of that sort. (The victim lived in an isolated house in the mountains and had little contact with others; nobody had seen her since February, so it wasn't unreasonable to assume that was when she had died.) I felt strongly that my suspect had committed the crime, but I kept running into this discrepancy between the assumed date of death (in February) and his return from Taiwan (in April). As a result, the case was never solved.

Now, looking back, I'd say the police doctor must have misjudged when the woman had died. As you know, the longer a body has been lying there, the harder it becomes to determine the exact time of death. Every doctor has a tendency to overshoot or undershoot the mark – what I believe is known these days as 'personal error'. Anyway, this particular doctor seems to have overestimated the time that had passed. The fact that the woman was wearing a padded jacket may also have swayed his judgement.

Even now, it will often occur to me that we do sometimes get cold days even in early April; to use another recently coined term, a 'cold front' can cause an unseasonal chill. Perhaps, on the day she was killed, the old woman felt so cold that she got her jacket back out from the cupboard. It strikes me as just the kind of thing an elderly person might do. The mere fact that she was wearing the jacket doesn't have to mean it was winter when she died. It could just as easily have been April. In other words, my suspect could have been the culprit after all.

But it was only much later that I came to this realization, and I can only regret failing to do so twenty years ago. If I had just stuck at it that little bit longer, I'm sure I would have cracked the case. Instead I was swayed by the doctor's assessment and that jacket, and the truth slipped from my grasp.

This is just one example, off the top of my head, from any number that I could mention. You see, I have many such regrets.

2

In other words, if everything is telling you this man is guilty, then you must comb through all the evidence a second time, and then a third. We all fall prey to preconceptions that make us take certain things for granted. This is a dangerous thing. Our slavish reliance on our own common sense creates a blind spot. I believe that, in an investigation, even the most elementary assumptions must be broken down and examined afresh.

In your recent letter you explained how Tatsuo Yasuda created witnesses to Sayama and Toki's departure from Tokyo station. I found this most interesting. I agree that it implies that Yasuda has a significant connection to the double suicide. Indeed, as you suggest, it seems highly likely that he was on the beach at Kashii that night and had a hand in these deaths.

What comes to my mind now is this. On the night of the double suicide, that is, the night of the twentieth of January, two separate couples disembarked at the two stations in Kashii. These two couples arrived at almost exactly the same time, before heading towards the beach. What if one couple was Sayama and Toki, and the other was Yasuda with *another woman*?

The next question would then be: what role was played by this other woman? In other words, if Yasuda was planning something involving the two lovers, why might he require a partner? Her involvement would suggest that Yasuda's plot could only be carried out by the two of them working together as a team. What could this mean?

After receiving your letter, I visited Kashii beach again. This time, I went in the evening. Unlike our previous visit, there was now a pleasant, cool breeze blowing. Perhaps that was why there were so many couples out for a walk. The city lights being some way off, these couples were nothing more than shadows in the night. If you'll allow me this comment at my age, it was probably this very darkness that made it the perfect spot for a pair of young lovers. Anyway, the point is that

Sayama and Toki, as well as Yasuda and the other woman, would have been mere shadowy forms as they made their way towards the beach on the night of the twentieth of January. It was so dark that if the distance between them had been more than six or seven metres, each couple would have been unaware of the other's presence. Unfortunately, at present, this is the limit of my meagre insight. But something tells me there is more to all this.

You also asked me to investigate the inns at which Yasuda might have stayed on the night of the twentieth. I have tried everything I can, but it has been rather a while since the night in question. What's more, many guests register themselves under fake names, while some inns wouldn't even deign to show me the register in the first place. Unfortunately, therefore, I have no leads at present. I will continue to investigate, but I have to say it is looking rather hopeless.

One other thought occurs to me: we have so far assumed that the woman who telephoned Sayama at the inn on the night of the twentieth was Toki, but what if, in fact, it was this other woman? Of course, this is a mere supposition, and I have no evidence to back it up. But if Yasuda had been in contact with Sayama and knew he would check in under the fake name of Sugawara, he could easily have told the other woman to ask for someone under that name when telephoning the inn. There's no reason why it had to be Toki making the call.

Taking this line of reasoning a little further, what if the woman Sayama spent a week waiting for at the Hakata inn was not Toki, his suicide partner, but rather the mystery woman? If that were the case, it would make sense if, as you suggest, Toki did not accompany Sayama all the way to Hakata, but instead left the train at Atami or Shizuoka. In short, could Toki's role simply have been to travel with Sayama part of the way? This might bring us closer to understanding Yasuda's motive in creating witnesses to Sayama and Toki's departure. Perhaps he simply wanted someone to see the two of them leaving Tokyo *together*, in good spirits. Why, I do not know. I have no concrete evidence to support this theory yet, and will need to give it further thought.

But if my deductions are correct, the next question would be where Toki went between getting off the train at Atami or Shizuoka and committing suicide in the bay of Kashii in Kyushu on the night of the twentieth. If we can only find that out, we will finally have evidence to support these speculations. As I explained during your visit, I believe that the receipt for 'one person' that was found in Sayama's jacket pocket makes it quite possible that Toki did not travel all the way to Hakata with Sayama.

If, as you suggest, we assume Yasuda's presence at the scene of the suicide on the night of the twentieth to be an absolute certainty, there is no way he could have arrived in Sapporo the following day if he travelled there on the Marimo Express. Despite this, you say there is no trace of him making the journey by plane. But this feels to me like a case of something being so obvious it is overlooked – another 'padded jacket' situation, if you will. I beg you to persevere, to go that extra mile I mentioned earlier. All it will take is one more push.

I must apologize. In my great joy at receiving your letter, I seem to have written at length about rather trivial matters and thrown in some senile ramblings for good measure. Compared to your sharp-witted self I am an ageing hack, and it embarrasses me to have got caught up in such digressions. Please, make of them what you will. And, if I can ever be of assistance from Fukuoka, do not hesitate to ask: I will do everything within my rather limited powers to help.

My hope is that, with your unceasing efforts, this complex case will soon be solved. And once it is, if ever you have the time, I would love to see you down here in Kyushu.

Yours,
Jūtarō Torigai

3

Mihara was exhausted. Walls were blocking his progress in every direction, and each seemed more unbreakable than the last.

With the long letter from Torigai tucked in his pocket, he left the police headquarters and headed for his usual café.

It was just past noon, and the café was bustling. While he was looking for a seat, a young woman invited him to share her table. She was sitting alone, drinking a cup of tea. The space opposite her was the only one available. Mihara felt uncomfortable sharing his table with a stranger and sat rather awkwardly on the edge of the chair while he drank his coffee. He was painfully aware how dejected he must look.

It was true that Torigai's letter had brought some consolation amid his gloom, but it hadn't exactly spurred him to action. Torigai's theories were too vague for that. Mihara was certainly intrigued by the idea of deducing, from the separate couples at the two Kashii stations on the night of the twentieth, the presence of an additional, mysterious woman. But, as Torigai himself admitted, there was simply no evidence to back this up. The couples might have had nothing to do with each other, having simply happened to leave the two stations at around the same time. Or perhaps there had only ever been one couple: Sayama and Toki, who had disembarked at the main Kashii station and then been spotted again as they walked past the Nishitetsu station. Torigai himself had measured the distance between the two stations and verified that this was entirely possible.

By now, Mihara was convinced that Yasuda had been on the beach that night and had played some part in the double suicide. But wasn't it going a little far to imagine, on top of that, the presence of a mysterious additional woman? Somehow, Mihara felt that Yasuda's task had required him to work alone. What that task had been was not yet clear, though he certainly had his suspicions.

As for Torigai's theory that the woman who called Sayama at the inn was not Toki, that too relied on the purely speculative notion that the four people at the two Kashii stations had been Sayama, Toki, Yasuda and this mysterious woman.

More interesting was Torigai's suggestion that the reason Yasuda had created witnesses to Sayama and Toki's departure was simply to provide convincing evidence that the two were intimate. Why would he do this? The only answer Mihara could think of was that, in fact, there had never been a romantic relationship between Sayama and Toki. In other words, it had been precisely to create the illusion of such a relationship that Yasuda had gone to such lengths to stage, for his witnesses, the spectacle of the pair merrily boarding the train together.

And yet, a few days later, not far from the train's destination of Hakata, Sayama and Toki had ended their lives together. It was a classic lovers' suicide, whichever way you looked at it. This didn't make sense: why would two people do such a thing if they weren't lovers? Somewhere in the midst of this contradiction, Mihara sensed Yasuda's looming presence.

There was also the question of why Toki might have got off at Atami or Shizuoka, but it was far from certain that she had even done so. Torigai had only deduced as much from the dining-car receipt for one person, basing his hypothesis on a subtle observation about how men and women behaved in relationships. The veteran detective's intuition was sharp, but he had identified no concrete evidence, instead venturing into the realm of speculation. He had suggested they investigate Toki's movements after she got off the train at Atami or Shizuoka, but that would not be easy at this late stage and nor was it even clear what it would achieve.

These were Mihara's thoughts as he glumly sipped his coffee. Just then, a shadow fell across the table. A young man had joined the woman.

'Sorry I'm late,' he said. The woman, who had seemed rather dispirited until now, beamed at her companion as though suddenly revitalized.

'What will you have?' she asked, glancing eagerly at him.

'A coffee.' The man gave the waitress his order, then turned to his companion with a smile. 'Have you been waiting a while?'

'Forty minutes or so. My coffee didn't last me, so I ordered a cup of tea.'

'I'm sorry,' said the young man. 'The bus was late. They're never on time on that route – they always show up twenty minutes after they're supposed to.'

'Well, if you're so sure it was the bus's fault!' the woman replied, smiling despite herself as she raised a slender wrist to consult her watch. 'It's starting soon. Drink up!'

Mihara listened absent-mindedly to this banal exchange between the young couple. In the time it took Mihara to light a cigarette, the young man drank a mouthful of his coffee and rose to leave, encouraging his companion to do the same.

Mihara, able to relax now, settled into his chair. Their cups remained on the table, one still full of coffee. The man must live quite far out of town if the buses were so unreliable, Mihara thought. His mind was drifting, occupied by thoughts that were, for his purposes, entirely useless.

Or were they? Mihara sat up with a start. An idea had occurred to him.

Yasuda had sent a telegram specifically asking Kawanishi to meet him in the waiting room at Sapporo station, rather than on the platform. What if he had done so because he was worried about bad weather delaying his plane?

Mihara was staring at an oil painting on the wall as though transfixed.

Yasuda's plan had been to arrive on the Marimo, so it would certainly have been more effective to have Kawanishi meet him on the platform. But he also knew that the planes were often delayed by a few hours due to the weather or technical problems. If that happened, he would have missed his connection with the Marimo in Otaru, in which case, if Kawanishi *had* been waiting on the platform, it would have been quite clear that Yasuda hadn't been on the train.

The ever-cautious Yasuda had thought even this far ahead. This had to be why he had asked Kawanishi to meet him in the waiting room.

Mihara's eyes shone with excitement. I've got you, he thought. In the end, Yasuda's cunning scheme had served only to reveal that he *had* taken the plane after all.

Mihara left the café in a buoyant mood. Outside, the sun was bright and fierce.

Wait. That telegram. Where had Yasuda sent it from?

4

First of all, thought Mihara, he needed to ascertain Yasuda's movements in Hokkaido. All these tricks he had played made it abundantly clear that he knew his actions would be scrutinized later. This was true certainly of his encounter with the Hokkaido government official on board the Marimo, but especially of his request that Kawanishi meet him at Sapporo station. According to Kawanishi, there had been no urgent reason for them to meet there.

Where, then, had that telegram been sent from? When Mihara had asked about it in Sapporo, Kawanishi had said he had already disposed of it, unfortunately without noting the place of dispatch.

Yasuda had left Fukuoka by plane on the morning of the twenty-first. Could he have sent the telegram from the Fukuoka or Hakata telegraph office, or perhaps from the airport before his flight? No, Yasuda was too cautious for that. He had probably dispatched it from Tokyo, just in case Kawanishi noticed the location of the sending office. He would have had plenty of time to do so at Haneda during the hour-long layover before his flight to Sapporo.

But no, that wouldn't make sense either. By the time he arrived at Haneda, he would have known whether the Sapporo plane was leaving on time. And if it was, he would be able to catch the Marimo from Otaru and there would be no reason to make Kawanishi stay in the waiting room. Again, it would have been much more effective to meet Kawanishi on the platform and be seen actually disembarking.

At this point Mihara got out his notebook. According to his notes, Kawanishi had said the following: 'The telegram was sent at the ordinary rate. I suppose I must have received it at around eleven o'clock on the twenty-first.'

It took about two hours for an ordinary telegram to reach Sapporo from Tokyo, so it must have been sent at around nine o'clock. But at that time Yasuda had been on the plane from Fukuoka to Tokyo. He would have been somewhere over Hiroshima or Okayama. There was no way he could have sent the telegram himself from Tokyo.

Then what about Fukuoka? It would probably take just over two hours to send a telegram from Fukuoka to Sapporo, so if he had sent it before the eight o'clock plane from Itazuke airport, it could plausibly have reached Kawanishi at around eleven o'clock.

Could he really have sent it from Fukuoka? It would have been unlike him to risk revealing his location like this. Still, Mihara decided to contact the Fukuoka Police and ask them to check all outgoing telegrams on the twenty-first.

Back at headquarters, Mihara told Kasai his plan.

'I think you might be on to something,' said Kasai, his features creasing into a smile. 'So that's why he had Kawanishi meet him in the waiting room. Yes, let's have the Fukuoka Police check the telegrams. Though I suppose even if Yasuda didn't send it from Tokyo himself, someone else could always have done so on his behalf.'

'Exactly. That's why I was going to propose we also check with the Tokyo telegraph offices.'

'Good,' replied Kasai, smiling again as he sipped his tea. 'Mihara, these café trips of yours have a habit of triggering brainwaves.'

'What can I say? The coffee must be good for me,' replied Mihara cheerfully.

'But if the telegram turns out to have been sent from Tokyo, that doesn't get us anywhere, does it? After all, why wouldn't it have been? If he sent it from Fukuoka, on the other hand, that would prove he'd been in the city, and we'd finally have him.'

'Actually,' Mihara cut in, 'even if it was sent from Tokyo, that would still be significant. He couldn't have sent it himself, so it would mean he had an accomplice. If so, I'd want to know who.'

'Couldn't he just have asked one of his employees to send it?'

'No, that's impossible.'

'Why's that?'

'It was two in the afternoon on the twentieth when Yasuda left the office, saying he was off to Sapporo. It would have made sense for an employee to send the telegram that day, but not at nine o'clock the next morning. These are the kind of tiny details that Yasuda thinks about – and he was fully aware we'd investigate him at some point.'

Their conversation ended here. But a few days later, the detectives assigned to the task reported that no telegraph office in the Tokyo area had handled Yasuda's message. The response from the Fukuoka Police was the same: neither the Fukuoka nor the Hakata telegraph office had any record of the telegram in question.

Mihara was at a loss. Every telegram had to be sent from *somewhere*. Where on earth had Yasuda sent this one from?

5

Once again, Mihara clapped his hand to his head.

There must be something wrong with him! Why hadn't he thought to check the receiving office? This case really was turning his brain into mush. Immediately, he asked the Sapporo Police to look into the matter. Their reply came the following day.

'The telegram in question was sent from Asamushi station in Aomori prefecture, at 8.50 a.m. on the twenty-first of January.'

Not Tokyo, not even Fukuoka, but Asamushi, of all places. On an express train, Asamushi was the last stop before the terminus at Aomori.

Mihara was baffled. But when he thought about it, perhaps it wasn't so surprising. Asamushi was on the Tokyo–Hokkaido route, after all. Mihara noted the time of dispatch: 8.50. According to the timetable, that was when the Towada Express from Ueno, Tokyo, would be leaving Asamushi station.

The guard must have sent the telegram at the request of a passenger on the train, Mihara realized. The Towada, which passed through Asamushi on the morning of the twenty-first, was exactly the train that Yasuda had said he was on. It connected with the Seikan ferry No. 17, and then to the Marimo Express from Hakodate to Sapporo.

So Yasuda really had been on the Towada, as he had claimed!

Mihara felt his grasp on the case loosening. The more he

investigated, the more he found to support Yasuda's story. He buried his face in his hands.

Just then, Kasai interjected: 'What makes you so sure it was Yasuda who sent the telegram?'

'What?' Mihara raised his head.

'You said it yourself. That you wanted to know who his accomplice was.'

Accomplice . . . Mihara stared at Kasai. 'Of course. Yes, now I remember!' said Mihara, perking up again.

'A detective forgetting his own words – now that's a first!' said Kasai with a chuckle.

Mihara picked up the telephone, called Ueno station, and asked for the guards' office.

'Hello? I'd like to know where I can find the guard who would have been working on the Towada Express between Sendai and Aomori.'

'They're all at this office,' came the reply.

Mihara took a police car and sped to Ueno station, where he approached the clerk on duty.

'The Towada Express, number 205, departing on the twentieth of January? Just a moment, please,' said the clerk, opening the duty roster. 'It was a guard named Kajitani. He should be in at the moment. Should I call him?'

'Yes, please.'

Mihara's chest pounded with anticipation. Soon the guard arrived. He must have been around thirty and seemed a bright sort.

'I don't remember the exact content of the telegram, but yes, I recall being asked to send one to Sapporo. We were passing by Kominato, near Asamushi. I believe it was the morning of the twenty-first. I don't remember being asked to send any other telegrams from there around that time.'

'Do you recall anything distinctive about the person who asked you to send it?' asked Mihara, praying that the guard would remember something.

'Let's see . . . He was travelling in one of the second-class sleepers.'

'Okay. Go on.'

'If my memory serves me, he was quite tall and slim.'

'Ah! Slim, you say? Definitely not a stout sort of man?' Mihara repeated his question calmly, though inside he was rejoicing.

'No – if anything, he was thin.' The guard's memory seemed to be gradually returning. 'And he was with another person.'

'Wait. There were two of them?'

'Yes. I remember checking their tickets; it was the slim man who showed me them. The other man seemed like he might be his superior. He came across as a little haughty, and the slim man was very deferential towards him.'

'And it was this subordinate who asked you to send the telegram?'

'That's right.'

The identity of the accomplice who sent Yasuda's telegram had been revealed. There was no doubt in Mihara's mind: the superior in question must have been Division Chief Ishida, of Ministry X. The slim man with him must have been one of his staff.

Until now, Mihara had been operating under the assumption that Ishida had travelled to Hokkaido alone. But, of course, it would have been quite normal for a government official of his rank to be accompanied by a subordinate.

Next, Mihara paid a visit to Ministry X and discreetly enquired who had accompanied Division Chief Ishida to Hokkaido on the twentieth of January.

The man's name was Kitarō Sasaki. He was the same assistant who had visited Kasai a few days earlier, under Ishida's orders, with the message that Yasuda had indeed travelled on the Marimo.

The next day, Mihara flew to Aomori.

One by one, he checked the passenger forms for the Seikan ferry on the twenty-first of January.

There was Ishida's name, together with that of Yasuda. But the name Kitarō Sasaki was nowhere to be seen. That could mean only one thing: that Sasaki had travelled under Yasuda's name.

The wall that had loomed over Mihara, blocking his progress, had finally crumbled. This time, victory was within his grasp!

All that remained was to work out why the passenger form bore Yasuda's handwriting. But now that he had come this far, surely that wouldn't be too difficult.

13. Kiichi Mihara's Report

I

Dear Inspector Torigai,

The hot summer days are here. Walking under the blazing sun, I feel as though my shoes might sink into the soft tarmac at any moment. When I get home from the office I like nothing better than to strip off, rinse myself in the tub, and sit back with one of the beers we keep chilling in the well. I almost find myself missing the icy winds that blew in from the Sea of Genkai that day when you showed me Kashii beach.

It has been some time since I was last able to write a letter so calmly. It was in February of this year that I first met you in Hakata. Six months have passed since I stood in that bay, shivering in the wind as you explained your theories. Looking back, the time seems to have flown by, but the investigation has kept me so busy that I have been unable to rest even a moment. Now, however, my mind is at peace – as tranquil, perhaps, as the sun in early autumn. No doubt this is because the case is now closed. This feeling of rest is all the more profound after a troublesome investigation like this one. I suppose I need not explain such things to a veteran of your standing. In any case, it is this sense of accomplishment that has inspired me to write to you. To do so is my duty; it is also my great pleasure.

In a previous letter, I explained that the greatest challenges in this case concerned Tatsuo Yasuda's trip to Hokkaido. Your kind response, telling me to persevere, was most encouraging in this matter. I can't tell you how it lifted my spirits.

Yasuda's seemingly cast-iron alibi – that he left Ueno station in Tokyo on the Towada on the twentieth of January, crossed to Hakodate on the Seikan ferry, then arrived into Sapporo on the Marimo at 8.34 the following evening – has been shattered. At first, a series of seemingly unbreakable walls blocked my progress: Yasuda had been introduced to a Hokkaido government official on board the Marimo; someone had met him at Sapporo station at the time of that train's arrival; and there was a passenger form filled out in his handwriting for the Seikan ferry. I particularly struggled with the passenger form. In every respect, Yasuda's story seemed watertight.

Meanwhile, I hadn't found a scrap of evidence for my theory that he had travelled by plane. Yasuda's name wasn't on the passenger lists for any of the three flights (from Tokyo to Fukuoka, Fukuoka back to Tokyo, and then Tokyo to Sapporo), nor had any fake names been used. All one hundred and forty-three of the passengers were found by our investigation to be real people, each of whom insisted they had boarded the plane in question. Unless Yasuda was a ghost, there was no way he could have been on those planes. Here again, Yasuda's claims appeared to be indisputable.

In short, his *presence* on the train to Hokkaido was firmly established, while his *absence* from the planes seemed equally beyond doubt.

However, I was suspicious of the fact that Yasuda had sent a telegram asking Kawanishi to meet him in the waiting room at Sapporo station. Eventually I inferred that he did so because he was worried about his flight being delayed. (You'll recall that, by taking the plane, Yasuda hoped to make it to Otaru in time to board the Marimo.) We found out where the telegram had been sent from. It turned out a passenger on the Towada had asked the guard to send it when the train was near Asamushi on the morning of the twenty-first. The guard remembered the passenger, and from his physical description we identified Division Chief Ishida of Ministry X, together with his assistant Kitarō Sasaki. It was Sasaki who had asked the guard to send the telegram.

That was when it all made sense. You see, the ferry passenger list bore the name of Ishida, but not that of Sasaki. I realized that the latter must have handed over a passenger form in Yasuda's name when he boarded the ship. It had been careless of us to assume Ishida had travelled alone. When we questioned Sasaki later on, we learned that Yasuda had prepared the passenger form two weeks in advance. You see, when you board the ship in Aomori, there are piles of these forms by the ticket window, just like those blank telegram forms they have at the post office. Anybody can take as many as they like. Yasuda asked Ishida to procure a form via one of his employees who was visiting Hokkaido on business, then filled it out and gave it back to him. I will come back to the relationship between Yasuda and Ishida. But the ploy enabling Yasuda's handwriting to appear on the form, which had us entirely baffled, turned out to have been this simple all along.

Thus we uncovered the truth behind Yasuda's trip to Hokkaido. Next was the mystery of the plane passenger lists, and here I realized that we were dealing with the opposite problem: having established his absence from the train, we now needed to prove his presence on the plane.

We decided to check the one hundred and forty-three passengers once more, this time focusing on their stated occupations. We used a specific criterion to narrow the list down to five or six individuals: we were looking for businessmen with close connections to Ministry X. Then we turned up the pressure on each of them, one by one, until three of them finally confessed.

Mr A from Tokyo to Fukuoka, Mr B from Fukuoka to Tokyo, and Mr C from Tokyo to Sapporo: these three individuals never actually boarded the planes in question. They couldn't keep their act up for ever; they knew we'd catch them out eventually. All three admitted that Mr Ishida had asked them, in confidence, to let him use their names. Apparently, he told them: 'I'm sending someone on top-secret government business, so if the police happen to ask, please tell them you were on the plane. I promise you won't have any trouble.'

This was right when the bribery scandal was blowing up, so the three of them assumed an official was making the trip in order to hush things up. Having dealt with the ministry themselves, they knew how these things worked. Indeed, it turns out Ishida did them various business favours in return.

And so Yasuda flew between Tokyo, Fukuoka and Sapporo using the names of Mr A, Mr B and Mr C. Why not just use a single alias? Because if we checked the passenger lists, his movements would be obvious and the game would be up. Yasuda never forgot that he would be thoroughly investigated and planned meticulously for every eventuality.

Now we had cracked his Hokkaido alibi and established his presence in Hakata. But there was still one problem – that of the witnesses at Tokyo station. These were the two waitresses who, on the fourteenth of January, saw Sayama and Toki boarding the Asakaze together. Or, should I say, who were *made to witness* this scene – by, of course, Yasuda.

The real relationship between Sayama and Toki remains unclear, and we have found no evidence that might enlighten us. Toki was a very discreet young woman and, though the waitresses at the Koyuki told us she might have had a lover, they couldn't be sure. It seems they weren't trying to protect her – they really didn't know. We'd heard that a man would often call Toki and ask her to meet him somewhere, but she never brought him back to her apartment. So it seemed she did have a secret lover, but nobody knew who he was. Of course, after the suicide in Kashii, it was only natural to assume that the lover was Sayama.

However, there was something odd here.

2

Why did Yasuda need someone to witness Sayama and Toki at the station? Was it simply to prove they had travelled to Kyushu on the Asakaze Express? If so, why choose the Asakaze in particular? Surely any Kyushu-bound train would have done the trick. In any case, the two of them committed suicide together in Kyushu, so there was really no doubt as to their destination. There must have been another reason.

Yasuda wanted his witnesses to see Sayama and Toki boarding the train together and went to great efforts to ensure they were there on the platform with him. His real aim was to make them deduce, from what they saw, that Sayama and Toki were in love.

This was rather strange. Why would he need them to infer such a thing?

After much thought, I arrived at the paradoxical conclusion that Sayama and Toki were never lovers. No other explanation seemed possible. And, precisely because they weren't lovers, Yasuda needed his witnesses to conclude that they were.

I had been most impressed by your intuition in deducing, from a single dining-car receipt, the fact that Sayama had travelled to Hakata alone. Your suspicions had been roused by the fact that the receipt was only for one person, while your daughter's insights into the likely behaviour of a young woman in love proved most enlightening. It seemed, then, that Toki must have left the train at some point along the way, while Sayama continued alone to Hakata. From all this, I concluded that Sayama and Toki were never lovers or indeed anything of the sort.

Yasuda was a regular customer at the Koyuki and often entertained his business contacts there. Sayama never visited the restaurant, but it seems he did know Toki. Perhaps the three of them – Yasuda, Sayama and Toki – had met up on occasion without anyone knowing. In any case, Sayama and Toki were at least acquainted with each other, so it was only natural for them to board the train together and strike up a conversation. To an uninformed witness, they would have been the spitting image of a pair of young lovers setting off on a trip together. This, of course, was Yasuda's intention.

It must therefore have been Yasuda who arranged for the two of them to board the same train. For a man in his position, this would have been easy to do.

But there was a problem. Yasuda's goal was to make the witnessing of the couple seem entirely accidental. Platform 15 is where the long-distance trains depart from, and insisting on taking the waitresses there could have seemed suspicious. Instead, he had to ensure they saw the couple from another platform. The most natural would be platform 13, serving the Yokosuka line, which he often used when visiting his wife in Kamakura. That way, his ruse would pass undetected.

Now he faced another problem. Standing on platform 13, it isn't normally possible to observe the trains at platform 15. As I explained in my previous letter, other trains are constantly arriving and departing on the tracks in between, blocking the view. But, after searching long and hard, Yasuda discovered that there was a four-minute window every day during which a Kyushu-bound train could be seen from platform 13. This was between 5.57 and 6.01. A mere four minutes – and yet, for Yasuda, a vital four minutes.

I mentioned above that surely any Kyushu-bound train would have sufficed, but now we can see why it had to be the 6.30 Asakaze Express. Yasuda had to make absolutely sure that they both boarded that train. Any other train for Kyushu and the view would have been blocked. This was a stroke of genius by Yasuda: identifying this four-minute window and serving it up to his witnesses as if it were the most natural thing in the world. Surely even among the employees of Tokyo station there must be few aware such an interval exists.

And so it became clear that Yasuda had staged Sayama and Toki's departure. But this failed to explain why, six days later, the pair went to the beach in Kashii, drank juice containing cyanide and died side by side. Though I only saw photographs of the scene, it was abundantly clear from the doctor's report and the way they were found that this was a double suicide.

Now, this I simply didn't understand. Why would two people who weren't lovers end their lives in this way? Even supposing Yasuda had ordered them to do so, surely no one would be mad enough to actually follow through on such a request! The clear fact of the double suicide seemed to demolish my theory that Sayama and Toki were not lovers; the only possible explanation was that they had, after all, been deeply in love. This was a contradiction that I simply could not resolve.

If their departure together had in fact been a ploy on the part of Yasuda, then it made little sense that they would really have committed suicide together on that beach. And yet there was no denying that that was precisely what had happened. Their journey had started in one way and ended in quite another, creating a discrepancy I could not unravel, no matter how much I racked my brains.

But, since Yasuda had plotted the beginning of this journey, I sensed that he also had a hand in its tragic denouement. This basic intuition, however vague, never left me. Even when I was investigating his trip to Hokkaido, I was unable to shake the feeling that Yasuda's shadow loomed large over the events on Kashii beach that night. What exactly he had done, I did not know. Surely, I thought, he hadn't hypnotized them into committing suicide together! And yet there was no way that two people in their right minds would commit suicide together simply because someone had ordered them to. I was at a loss, and yet I decided, against the evidence, to persist in my conviction that he had been present that night.

We had managed to break Yasuda's Hokkaido alibi and establish that on the twentieth of January he had travelled by plane from Tokyo to Hakata, leaving Haneda at 3.00 and arriving at Itazuke at 7.20. Thus, he could have been on Kashii beach at around 10 p.m. – the time of the double suicide. But, when it came to linking Yasuda to those deaths, I ran up against a wall. Try as I might, I could come up with nothing. I was in despair.

One day, in the midst of this desperation, I happened to visit a café. I am quite the coffee drinker, you know. The chief likes to poke fun at me for it, but by this point I was feeling so wretched that I needed to get out of the office. There's a café in Ginza I usually visit, but as it was raining I thought I'd try a nearby spot in Hibiya instead.

The café was spread over two floors. When I went to open the door, a young woman arrived from the other direction at just the same moment. We almost bumped into each other, and then, out of politeness, I let her enter first. She was very pretty and wore a brightly coloured raincoat. She smiled and bowed slightly to me before walking into the café and handing her umbrella to the waitress at the bottom of the stairs. I followed her, but when I tried to give my own umbrella to the waitress, she assumed we were a couple, tied our umbrellas together, and held out a single numbered ticket with which to collect them later. The young lady blushed slightly, and I hastened to explain: 'No, no – we're not together. We just got here at the same time!'

The waitress apologized, separated our umbrellas and handed me a different ticket.

3

You are perhaps wondering why I am bothering to relate this mix-up, flattering though it may have been. In fact, this arbitrary incident triggered a revelation. It came as a shock – a real light-bulb moment. I walked up to the second floor in a daze, and it was some time before I even noticed the coffee I'd ordered on the table in front of me.

You see, the girl at the entrance had assumed we were a couple because we walked into the café together. That was only natural. Anyone would have drawn the same conclusion. Knowing nothing about us, she made this assumption on the spur of the moment simply because she saw us walk in one after the other. This led me to an important realization.

We all – including, I'm afraid, yourself and the other good officers of the Fukuoka Police – concluded that we were dealing with a double suicide because Sayama and Toki were found lying side by side. Now, I realized that the two must have died separately – and in different places. It was only after their death that their two bodies were moved to a single location. Someone made Sayama drink cyanide, he collapsed, and next to his body was placed that of Toki, who had been made to ingest the same poison. Sayama and Toki died separately, but when we saw them side by side our own preconceptions took over and we assumed they had ended their lives together.

People might laugh at the idea that just because a man and woman were found lying almost in each other's arms they should immediately be assumed to have committed a love suicide. And yet, since time immemorial, thousands upon thousands of couples have been found in just such a state, without anybody suspecting foul play. Once their deaths are deemed a love suicide, the inquest is never as thorough as it would be for a murder. The investigation becomes a well-rehearsed affair. This was precisely what Yasuda sought to exploit.

I remember what you wrote in your letter to me. 'We all fall prey to preconceptions that make us take certain things for granted. This is a dangerous thing. Our slavish reliance on our own common sense creates a blind spot.' This was precisely what had happened here. A man and a woman died together, and our minds, dulled by various preconceived notions, jumped to the conclusion that it was a love suicide. We had been blinded by the obvious; the criminal had used our own assumptions against us.

But this double suicide would hardly be plausible unless Yasuda could convince us that Sayama and Toki, who in fact barely knew each other, had secretly been lovers. This was why, at Tokyo station, he made sure the waitresses from the Koyuki got a good look at the two of them happily boarding the train together. Yes, Yasuda had gone as far as fabricating evidence of a relationship. A criminal is always beset by endless worries, but the meticulous Yasuda left nothing to chance. And eventually, he discovered his precious four-minute interval.

Looking back now, I see that, from start to finish, this case was only ever a matter of train and plane timetables. The answers all lay buried within them. I even found myself wondering whether this was some personal interest of Yasuda's. I couldn't shake the feeling that all this could only have been the work of someone with an odd passion for such things. Let us set to one side the problem of Sayama and Toki's deaths and focus on this question of timetables.

Now, a certain woman comes vividly to my mind. This woman was a veritable connoisseur of the train timetable. She even wrote an essay on the subject for a magazine. In that essay, brimming with poetic sentiment, she explained that these columns of numbers, so seemingly mundane to the uninitiated, could be more absorbing than any novel. To her they were an endless source of inspiration, the starting point for many a mental voyage. Confined to her bed by tuberculosis, she found in the train timetable all the faithful companionship of a Bible and all the fascination of a great work of literature. This woman was Yasuda's wife. Her name was Ryōko, and she was convalescing in Kamakura.

It is said that those suffering from tuberculosis often develop an over-active imagination. So, what thoughts did the pale-faced Ryōko pursue? Or rather, what plots did she hatch? Something tells me that, seemingly lost in contemplation, she was really spinning her own web of intersecting lines between these endless columns of numbers. At this point, it dawned on me that perhaps none of this had ever been Yasuda's idea. What if, instead, the real mastermind had been Ryōko?

And then I remembered those two couples, at the two stations, that night in Kashii. One couple, of course, was Sayama and Toki. What if the other had been Yasuda and his wife, Ryōko? This was a natural enough deduction, and one, I soon realized, that was only half wrong . . .

You wrote in your letter: 'The next question would then be: what role was played by this other woman? In other words, if Yasuda was planning something involving the two lovers, why might he require a partner? Her involvement would suggest that Yasuda's plot could only be carried out by the two of them working together as a team.'

I now found myself agreeing with you entirely. Once I had realized that this woman might have been Yasuda's wife, I decided to investigate her further.

But Ryōko was a bedridden invalid. She might well have planned the crime, but could she really have helped execute it too? In other words, had she been in any condition to travel from Kamakura all the way to Kyushu?

I went back to Kamakura and questioned her doctor again. He had previously told me Ryōko was not completely confined to bed and sometimes visited relatives in Yugawara. When I asked about her possible movements around the twentieth of January, he checked her medical records and confirmed that she had been away from the nineteenth to the twenty-first. The doctor usually visits Ryōko twice a week and happened to have seen her on the twenty-second. Ryōko had a temperature that day. When he asked her if she knew why, she told him: 'I went to Yugawara on the nineteenth and came back this morning. I must have overdone it slightly.'

This is it, I thought. If she had left on the evening of the nineteenth, she could have arrived in Hakata the next day. In other words, she could have been at the scene of the double suicide. The trip to Yugawara must have been a lie, and her real destination Kyushu.

Next, I managed to speak discreetly to Ryōko's elderly maid. I grilled her until she eventually revealed that Ryōko had left for Yugawara at around two o'clock on the afternoon of the nineteenth, in a rented car. So I tracked down the driver.

4

The driver told me Ryōko had indeed asked him to take her to Yugawara. But when they arrived, she told him to carry on to Atami, where he dropped her in front of the Kaifusō inn before returning to Kamakura.

At this, I practically jumped for joy. Needless to say, I immediately rushed to Atami to ask questions at the Kaifusō. Here is what I found out.

Ryōko had visited a female guest who was staying in the 'Kaede' room. The woman in question had arrived alone at around half past eight on the fourteenth of January and stayed at the inn for five days. Based on her age and appearance, it was clear this woman was Toki. It came as no surprise that she had registered under a fake name, but what was interesting was the one she used: Yukiko Sugawara. You'll recall that Sugawara was also the alias used by Sayama at the inn in Hakata. When she arrived at the Kaifusō, Ryōko had asked for Mrs Sugawara. It was clear, then, that all this had been agreed in advance between Sayama, Toki and Ryōko – or perhaps it would be more accurate to say that Ryōko had planned the whole thing. The two women had dinner in the room, before leaving the inn at around ten at night. It was Ryōko who paid Toki's bill.

Now, the fact that Toki arrived at the inn at around eight thirty on the fourteenth confirms that she arrived on the Asakaze. That train reaches Atami at 7.58, so she must have travelled that far with Sayama from Tokyo. In other words, your theory of the dining-car receipt 'for one' was right on the mark.

Toki and Ryōko left the inn at about 10 p.m. on the nineteenth. I looked at the timetable and saw that the Tsukushi

Express, bound for Hakata, departed from Atami at 10.25. It reached Hakata, its final destination, at 7.45 the following evening – that is, on the twentieth.

Everything was falling into place. After all, hadn't it been eight o'clock in the evening when a woman phoned Sayama at the Tambaya inn in Hakata? In other words, she had called Sayama shortly after getting off the train.

This much I had worked out, but I was at a loss as to what happened next. Was it Toki or Ryōko who made the phone call? Of course, at first we assumed it must have been Toki, but that no longer made sense. If Sayama and Toki had no relationship to speak of, why would he leave the inn at her request? And why would he have waited anxiously for a whole week in Hakata for her to phone?

No, it was more plausible for Ryōko to have made the call. She was Yasuda's wife and could act as his proxy. In other words, it was *Yasuda's* arrival that Sayama had been waiting for. This was why, hearing that Ryōko had come in her husband's stead, he rushed out to join her.

The two of them met, and Ryōko promised to discuss the matter Sayama had been agonizing about – but only once they had reached Kashii beach. Under what pretext she convinced him to go to the beach, I do not know. Perhaps she told him a deserted location like that would let them talk more freely. In any case, Kashii beach was an important part of the plan.

Of course, it was the ongoing corruption case that was weighing on Sayama's mind. As assistant section chief, he knew all about the ministry's inner workings, and it was only a matter of time before he would be dragged into the investigation's net. It was Division Chief Ishida who persuaded Sayama to take a 'break' from his duties and seek refuge in Hakata. Ishida was a key suspect in the corruption investigation, and Sayama's arrest would put him in serious danger. So he made Sayama bow to the inevitable and flee to Hakata. He even told him which train to take: the Asakaze Express, on the fourteenth of January. 'Yasuda will come to Hakata with further instructions,' he told him. 'Until then, lie low at the inn.'

Sayama had followed these orders to the letter. And who can blame him? He knew that any testimony he gave could end up causing trouble for Ishida, the benevolent superior who had taken him under his wing. Most assistant section chiefs would have done the same. Some have even committed suicide in situations like this. Indeed, it was precisely this possibility that the criminals sought to exploit.

Ishida told Sayama that Yasuda would find a way to cover up the scandal, and for now he was simply to sit tight. Sayama therefore waited anxiously for Yasuda to arrive. In the end, however, it was Ryōko who came on Yasuda's behalf. Sayama knew her from visiting the Yasuda residence in Kamakura. In fact, I believe Yasuda may even have invited Sayama to Kamakura purely to ensure the two were acquainted.

Sayama and Ryōko got off the train at the main Kashii station, unaware that shortly afterwards Yasuda and Toki would arrive at the Nishitetsu station and make their way towards the same beach. Or rather, Sayama was unaware. Ryōko knew perfectly well what was happening.

Ryōko talked with Sayama and reassured him that everything was going to be fine. She offered him some whisky, perhaps telling him it would stave off the cold. Sayama, a keen drinker, was grateful for the whisky and gulped it down. It contained cyanide. He collapsed on the spot. The bottle of poisoned juice found at the scene was a red herring planted by Ryōko.

Yasuda and Toki arrived shortly afterwards. Yasuda had landed at 7.20 on a flight from Tokyo, before collecting the young waitress from a pre-arranged location; Ryōko must have told Toki where to meet him. Now he escorted her to the beach. As they walked, a passer-by overheard her say: 'What a lonely place.'

On that gloomy, deserted beach, Yasuda made Toki, too, drink whisky laced with cyanide. Once she had fallen to the ground, he picked her body up and laid it next to Sayama's; he had already stopped breathing. Ryōko would have been standing by his body. Toki probably died less than twenty metres from where Sayama already lay but, in that darkness, she would not have seen a thing.

After he'd killed Toki, I imagine Yasuda called out to his wife:

'Ryōko?'

From the darkness, Ryōko must have replied:

'Over here!'

And Yasuda must have picked up Toki's body and carried it in the direction of his wife's voice, to where Sayama's body lay. A grimmer scene I cannot imagine.

Now let us consider their surroundings. You showed me the area yourself, so you know that Kashii beach is a rocky place. Even someone carrying a heavy load would leave no footprints. The criminals had planned everything meticulously. Yasuda must have known about the beach in advance, and thus chose it as the scene of the murder.

This murder in the guise of a love suicide was the joint handiwork of the Yasudas. Ryōko didn't just plan the crime; she helped carry it out.

Toki, meanwhile, had followed the couple's instructions without suspecting a thing. Now, the relationship between her and the Yasudas had been puzzling me. As you may have guessed from the above, it seems Tatsuo Yasuda and Toki were having an affair. They must have kept a very tight lid on their relationship; it seems no one else knew about it. They had got to know each other during Yasuda's visits to the Koyuki, where Toki always waited on him. The man who phoned her from time to time, and with whom she spent nights away from home, was none other than Yasuda.

But in this case Ryōko's behaviour seemed strange. Toki was her husband's mistress and by rights her rival. How could they have been on friendly enough terms to meet up in Atami and board the train together?

Then I recalled that Ryōko had paid for Toki's stay at the inn there, and it all fell into place. She had known about the affair all along. Indeed, she had given it her approval: it turns out she was paying Toki a monthly allowance from her own pocket. Remember, Ryōko's illness had made her weak; her doctor had forbidden her from having any sexual relations with her husband. In a manner of speaking, then, Toki was Ryōko's authorized stand-in. Quite the twisted relationship, and indeed one we may find hard to fathom. But such things are not unheard of. In the old feudal days, I believe it was even common practice.

At first, the Yasudas probably intended to stage only a single suicide, that of Sayama. But this would have been too risky. With no suicide note, his death would arouse suspicion. This was when they hit on the idea of a love suicide. In such cases, the investigation is less thorough, and nor is there any detailed autopsy or inquest. All told, it's a remarkably convenient way of murdering someone. Poor Toki, meanwhile, had the misfortune of being chosen as Sayama's suicide partner.

Yasuda was not particularly attached to Toki. He would have no trouble finding someone else to take care of his physical needs. As for Ryōko, she had never seen Toki as anything more than a tool for her husband; now she became one for staging a suicide. Still, deep down, Ryōko must have despised her. Ryōko was a woman to be feared. Her mind was as sharp as a razor; her blood as cold as ice. She was meticulous down to the last detail, smoothing out Toki's ruffled kimono and replacing her dirty tabi socks with a clean pair to suggest that Toki had been ready and willing to die.

The criminals stayed in Hakata that night. In the morning, Yasuda took the first plane to Tokyo and then flew on to Hokkaido, while his wife returned to Kamakura by train.

As for Yasuda's decision to wait six whole days before heading to Fukuoka, this was because he didn't want to attract suspicion by leaving Tokyo too soon after Sayama and Toki. He even showed up at the Koyuki for a few evenings after the fourteenth, looking nonchalantly on as the waitresses discussed Toki's trip with her lover. He wanted to make it abundantly clear that none of this had anything to do with him. This was why he made Toki, too, wait five days at the inn in Atami.

In this way, Tatsuo Yasuda, acting at the behest of his close ally, Division Chief Ishida, succeeded in liquidating Assistant Section Chief Sayama. In so doing, he put Ishida clear of danger. And not just Ishida: plenty of Sayama's other superiors will have breathed a sigh of relief at the news of his death. Meanwhile, Yasuda, a major machinery dealer, had bought himself a huge amount of favour with Ishida.

You see, it turns out Yasuda and Ishida had a much cosier relationship than any of us had imagined. Yasuda had been using every trick in the book to ingratiate himself with Ishida and thereby boost his company's trade with the ministry. You know the kind of thing: gifts, entertainment, lavish meals. The ongoing bribery scandal has made it patently clear that Ishida is the type to look kindly on such attention. Because Yasuda and Ishida's business dealings had so far been fairly limited, we failed to notice that, underneath the surface, Yasuda was working all his distinctive charm on Ishida in a bid to secure himself a rosy future. And indeed, it seems he succeeded in cultivating a clandestine, intimate relationship with the division chief. Knowing that Ishida feared getting caught up in the corruption investigation, Yasuda took on the task of eliminating the man who had become the crux of the entire investigation: Assistant Section Chief Sayama. Indeed, it may well have been Yasuda who talked Ishida into the idea.

Now, I do not believe Ishida ever wanted Sayama killed. Rather, he thought they could pressure him into committing suicide, like so many hapless underlings before him. But this proved impossible, and it was at this point that Yasuda had the idea of dressing his murder up as a suicide. Next, it struck him that a *double* suicide would be even more convincing. If Sayama were to be found dead on his own, people might still suspect murder, but dying alongside his supposed lover would arouse far less suspicion. Yasuda had found a trick that would throw us right off the scent.

Ishida, meanwhile, had no idea Yasuda intended to actually kill Sayama. He went along with Yasuda's idea because he thought the plan was simply to pressure the assistant section chief into committing suicide. He organized the business trip to Hokkaido, obtained the blank forms for the Seikan ferry, and arranged the fake passengers on the planes. As a high-ranking official at the ministry, he was free to travel whenever he liked, and could easily take along an assistant who would do his bidding.

But when he heard that both Sayama *and his lover* had committed suicide using cyanide, he must have turned white as a sheet. He would have known then that Yasuda had killed them. Now I believe the tables turned, and Yasuda could begin to exert pressure on Ishida. No doubt the division chief started to panic. It was probably at Yasuda's insistence that he sent his assistant, Kitarō Sasaki, to the Tokyo Police with the statement confirming that the Hokkaido trip had indeed taken place. Of course, that ended up backfiring; the statement in question contributed to Yasuda's downfall.

Yasuda had grown tired of Toki and saw in her simply a means of getting rid of Sayama. But what about Ryōko? I believe that the prospect of killing the young waitress may have been what really drew her to the plan, rather than simply the opportunity to help her husband. Yes, she had agreed to Toki acting as her stand-in, but deep down she never stopped seeing the waitress as a rival. Physically unable to satisfy her husband, Ryōko burned with a secret jealousy of uncommon intensity. When this opportunity for vengeance came along, that pale, phosphorus-like flame was stoked until it positively roared. I believe that Toki, even more than Sayama, was the real victim in this sorry affair. By the end, even Yasuda may not have known whether his primary motive was killing Sayama to buy favour with Ishida, or simply getting rid of Toki because she had become a burden.

Seichō Matsumoto

Everything I have written here has been based either on my own deductions, or on the suicide note left by the Yasudas.

Yes. Tatsuo and Ryōko Yasuda died at their home in Kamakura, just before we could arrest them. They had both taken cyanide. This time, there was nothing staged about the deaths.

Yasuda knew we had him cornered. And so he took his own life, followed by his wife, whose condition was worsening anyway. Yasuda left no note; it was Ryōko who penned the letter we found. In it, she claims they died consumed by guilt. I have to say I am not fully convinced. For one thing, I find it hard to imagine someone as tough as Yasuda committing suicide. It seems plausible that Ryōko, knowing her body would give up on her soon anyway, might have again resorted to some kind of trickery to take her husband with her to the grave. That is the kind of woman she was.

In truth, however, the death of the Yasudas came as a relief. Why? Because there was almost no material evidence against them. Everything we had was merely circumstantial. It's a wonder we even secured a warrant for their arrest. If this had gone to court, there's no telling what the outcome might have been.

Nor was there much for us to pin on Division Chief Ishida. Of course, after the bribery scandal he was transferred to a different division, but I hear his new position is even better than his old one. Absurd, I know, but then government ministries are absurd places. There's no telling what he might go on to become: a bureau chief? A vice-minister? Perhaps even a member of the Diet. The ones we should feel sorry for are his loyal subordinates: to Ishida, they're nothing but stepping stones on his way to the top. And yet, as long as they think he's looking out for them, they'll keep slaving away on his behalf. Yes, careerism is a depressing thing. As for Kitarō Sasaki, who acted as Ishida's assistant and Yasuda's accomplice – he's been promoted to section chief. And, with the Yasudas dead, all we can do is sit and watch.

This whole case leaves a sour taste in my mouth. Even now, relaxing at home with that cold beer I mentioned, I don't quite feel the sense of satisfaction I usually gain from solving a case and handing the culprit over to the public prosecutor.

This has been rather a long letter. I hope I haven't bored you.

Next autumn, work permitting, I plan to take you up on your kind offer and visit you in Kyushu with my wife.

Please accept my warmest wishes – and do take care of yourself.

Yours,
Kiichi Mihara

Note: All train and plane times mentioned in this work are taken from the timetables of 1957, the year in which the incident took place.